FROM
LONELY
Loved TO

ANNIE WOLTER

From Lonely to Loved

©2023 by Annie Wolter

www.anniewolter.com

ISBN 979-8-9854484-0-5

Published by Gem City Creations, Baraboo, Wisconsin 53913
www.gemcitycreations.com

Song lyrics copyright Annie Wolter:

"Gotta Get My Love in Your Heart" (2005)
"Older Brother Blues" (2005)
"Kimberly's Place" (2007)
"Man's Touch" (2017)
"The World of You" (2012)

Copyediting, Interior Design, and Cover Design by Michelle Rayburn
www.missionandmedia.com

This book is dedicated to *singles* everywhere that want to find a *life companion*.

FROM
LONELY
Loved TO

Trials and Triumphs
on my Faith Journey
toward Marriage

ANNIE WOLTER

GEM CITY CREATIONS

CONTENTS

Introduction: A Crisis of Dreams   1

1   The Best Christmas Gift Ever   3

2   Freedom for Fifteen?   13

3   A One-Moment, Forever Decision   25

4   Was God Calling Me to Be Single?   29

5   Let It Snow   37

6   The Challenge   43

7   Superstition   51

8   Pouring Out My Heart   57

9   Special Guy Friends   61

10   Gilman House   69

11   Learning to Better Love Myself   73

12   A Gift from Heaven   79

13   Therapist Failure   83

14   Praising God through the Pain   87

15   Jealousy, Misery   91

16   Jacob Wept Aloud   97

17   You Think You're Too Old, but God . . .   101

18   Patience, Donkey, Patience   111

19   The Five Sobs   115

20   An Awakening   119

21   Kimberly's Place   123

22   Midlife Crisis   127

23   Making Dreams into Goals   135

24   Therapist Success   145

25   What a Nice Kid   151

26   What a Nice Man   159

27   From a Dreamer's Point of View   167

28   Jacob Kissed Rachel   177

29   If You Must Know   183

30   Foam Core and Christmas Lights   189

31   From a Lover's Point of View   195

Acknowledgments   203

About the Author   205

A CRISIS OF DREAMS

As a young adult, I wanted to marry at age twenty-four, and when that didn't happen, I proved my flexibility by moving the goal to age twenty-six! When I turned twenty-*eight* with no dating prospects in sight. I experienced a painful crisis of dreams. It was hurtful to be so close to age thirty without time to meet someone, fall in love, get engaged, and have my first child before I passed that significant milestone.

Even though I was a devoted Christian, I hadn't been praying much about this dream, mostly because I had kept it as just that, a dream but not a goal. For years, I was victim to a myth that I had to be content living my life as a single person before God would send love my way.

One night, I finally cried out to God in my pain. I asked him to speak to me, no matter his answer, and let me know what the future held for me regarding marriage. That was the first time I asked God to actually talk to me about my love life, and he responded by giving me a promise that love would come to my door one day. But for now, there was a barrier. I didn't know how long he was talking about, and if I had known, I might have been discouraged.

All the waiting made sense in the end. There *had* been a barrier when my husband and I first met. Over time it resolved, and eventually we married.

I've written our story because some singles, looking for a lifelong love, are encouraged when they hear of our romance and receive hope that there is a divine purpose behind the waiting. They are at least encouraged that it's possible to find love at any point in life—even if it takes longer than hoped.

My goal is also to share and relate to the challenges, decisions, opportunities, and joys that can make up the milestones of anyone's path to marriage and to show how God listens, responds, and moves in our lives when we pour out our hearts to him. Finally, I hope to set people free from misplaced barriers that stop them from pursuing marriage as a goal.

Of course, not every unattached adult is looking for love. Many are content enjoying the richness of their present lives and too busy to get distracted by dreams of marriage, as my husband was. I understand. To you I offer a good love story and a book to pass onto a friend who could use its message.

But if you are in my target audience—if you want to get married or if you have repressed the desire because someone else convinced you to give up your dream and be content instead, or for any myriad of other reasons, I encourage you to be open to the idea of *making marriage a goal.*

My goal is also to share and relate to the challenges, decisions, opportunities, and joys that can make up the milestones of anyone's path to marriage and to show how God listens, responds, and moves in our lives when we pour out our hearts to him. Finally, I hope to set people free from misplaced barriers that stop them from pursuing marriage as a goal.

Happy reading!

One

THE BEST CHRISTMAS GIFT EVER

Age nine. It was the best of Christmases; it was the worst of Christmases. In 1970, I experienced a holiday dilemma like none before or since. It was a Christmas with virtually no presents. But out of that dark day, I experienced a joy like no other, one I can never forget and that still brings tears to my eyes. But my path to receiving that bliss was a challenging, difficult choice my mother had lovingly laid before me. She gave me an option—with no coercion—that I took. It was like a "Let's Make a Deal" secret curtain, ugly and unappealing, the one you didn't want to choose. But when it lifted, hiding behind it was the grand prize, the best Christmas gift ever!

Everything about my upbringing, my home, and the way our family celebrated Christmas had laid the foundation for me to make the fruitful choice that day. Let's start with the way my parents welcomed me into the world.

In the twenty-first century, a new baby is heralded long before its birth with a big gender reveal party (is it a boy or a girl?). However, for my parents, as a couple who had all their kids mid-twentieth century, the gender reveal came at the moment of the first spank (yes, they used to do that) and cry of the newborn. At least for my mom it did. Dad had to wait for the phone call.

And when they both knew I was a girl, they began calling me by the name they had chosen, Ann Marie. Choosing both Ann and Marie for my name earned my mother extra credit in the unofficial competition of Catholic mothers to creatively name their girls after Mary the mother of Jesus. Mom had given me the French version of Mary and also the name of Jesus's grandmother, Saint Anne, and that surely got her a few bonus points.

By the way, my older sister's first name was Mary (how could it be otherwise?), and my little sister was named Barbara Mary, so all my mother's girls received the name Mary. Of course, if any of us had been born in Mexico, our names might have included some form of both Mary and Jesus, totally outdoing the efforts of all Catholic mothers north of the border.

Historically, the ground had been laid for our names long before my seven siblings and I were born, back when my parents decided to get each of their children off to a good start with a solid Catholic name. My folks deeply appreciated the examples of those who had demonstrated a strong faith, as any Christian would, so we were all named after a canonized saint.

While I eventually chose to live out my faith as a Protestant, I cherish my upbringing and the foundation of faith my parents' devotion afforded me.

And so it was that the eight siblings were given sixteen saintly names: Thomas James, Paul Francis, George Michael, Mary Teresa, Patrick John, Michael Edward, Ann Marie, and Barbara Mary (last and far from least). Based on my parents' original goal, at my birth, they would have been at six kids down, six kids to go. Yes, they believed in "cheaper by the dozen." Ah, but it was not to be. In the end, they achieved only two-thirds of their goal: eight soundly named children born into their big fat Irish Catholic family.

My parents strived to live out their faith as strongly as they could in the traditions that were normal for their time. And then some. They didn't just take us to church every Sunday, send us to Christian schools, and have us receive all the sacraments our ages allowed. Much to our suffering, we were the only children in our neighborhood—and probably in the whole world, we thought—whose parents insisted on praying the entire rosary after dinner every night. Truly, I've never met anyone outside of our family who was raised this way.

No friends wanted to come to our house for supper because dessert was followed by twenty minutes of sheer sitting-still torture. Throughout the year, there were even special feasts when, for some reason, it was decided we should kneel through the prayers in spite of our linoleum flooring. Ouch!

In addition to these outward demonstrations of faith, more importantly, my parents worked hard to instill in us an appreciation for the Christian concepts of faith, forgiveness, and the unfathomable love of Jesus. When we received a new toy, we were encouraged—even required—to share it with our siblings. When we hurt, we prayed. And when we quibbled, Mom would begin to sing, "And they'll know we are Christians by our love . . ."

They applied these principles to bigger issues, too, such as modeling how to respond to negative events that happened in our neighborhood. This brings us to the story of the best Christmas gift ever.

Christmas always meant a lot of presents around the tree despite our being low income. Mom and Dad gave each of us four or five gifts, mostly toys, and required us to give a present to each of our other siblings. We were expected to use some of our weekly allowance for this, and my parents supplemented our funds where needed.

Even back in 1965, when I was so young that I couldn't read, I remember going to the Osco Drug store across the street from our home and finding a pretty little book for a quarter to give to my sixteen-year-old brother Paul. I knew he loved to read. It was a bedazzling Christmas-red, pocket-sized, three square inches of a book with gold scrolled letters. I was excited to find a book so beautiful to give him that I could afford. Most of the books were priced at three dollars or higher (yes, because they were *real books*; this was just a booklet, but not to my little eyes).

I couldn't read and had no idea of its contents, but I couldn't wait to give it to my brother because I knew no one could resist this one-of-a-kind book! And my brother did love it. In fact, he told me decades later how it fed his precocious teenage spirit so much that he carried it around in his pocket for two years. What was the book? On Christmas Day

My husband and I have enjoyed comparing our Catholic and Lutheran mothers' approaches to parenting. His also sang to him and his siblings a song about Christian love when they quarreled. And both of our moms banished the word "fart" from our vocabularies. His mom wins the prize for her efforts on this because she additionally charged them a dime anytime the word "fart" squeaked out of them (pun intended).

that year, teenager Paul opened from me, his preschool sister, a booklet called *Harvey Wallbanger's Guide to Mixed Drinks.*

But Christmas 1970 was different from the usual celebration. It's the only one I can remember for which there was so little money that Mom and Dad did not give us toys. Not one. Even though they had warned us that the Christmas gifts would be sparse and wouldn't include toys, it wasn't until I had opened my parents' presents that I fully felt the impact. I can still remember the sadness in my heart after I opened three or four gifts of clothes, and that was it. Even sibling gifts didn't bring forth a toy. Not old enough to appreciate gifts of apparel, I was stumped. What happened to Christmas?

> I can still remember the sadness in my heart after I opened three or four gifts of clothes.

Suddenly that day, a light shone in my darkness. By that year, my brother George was nineteen years old and had a good enough job to afford quality gifts. But that didn't diminish his procrastination in wrapping his gifts. And so, after all hopes for a toy had dwindled, he showed up with a last present and watched with delighted eyes as I opened it. Salvation. It was a game! Not just any game but one that my hyperactive mind would enjoy over and over again.

It was Battling Tops. Four players would wrap a thin string around their uniquely colored top, set the top in its launch chute, and then pull the string to send it spinning into a bright blue plastic arena to fight it out against the other tops until the last top was standing, the grand winner of the battle. I'd be able to pull all four strings myself if I had to! I couldn't wait for breakfast to come and go so I could dig into this game. In addition to the toy, George had taped a brand new one-dollar bill to the top of the box. Since it was 1970, I'd be able to buy ten candy bars with that money to keep my body in a sugar-crazed state for three full days.

We sat down to eat, and I felt okay. I was going to make it through the holiday with my one new toy. There was something to play with after breakfast and candy bars to buy as soon as the stores opened the next day.

But this solace ended as our Christmas breakfast finished. My mother shared her concern for the neighbors in the next block who had experienced a tragic home fire the night before. "Kids, I know we've had a difficult Christmas, but in all honesty, our neighbors have had a hit worse than ours. Not only did their Christmas tree burn, but so did all their gifts, and they are dealing with a burned out living room.

"So, here's what we are going to do as a family. I would like each of you to select one of your new Christmas gifts to give to our neighbors. I'm putting a box by the front door. Sometime today, I'd like you to put a gift in the box. It's up to you to decide what you want to give."

Yep, there she was again, modeling how to be Christ in our community.

As I left the table and went to sit in the living room by my new Christmas gifts, I was perplexed. Most of my gifts were clothes selected just for me in my size, and I didn't think that family had a girl. We really didn't know them well. And if they did, what if she was a different age or size than me? I had a cool game that anyone would want to play, but how could I give my only toy? I warily watched as my mother placed an empty box on a chair near the front door.

After a while, still unsure what to do, I asked her, "Mom, which gift should I give?" I expected her to come to my side and peruse my gifts with me. She would figure out the best approach. She would probably tell me to give the socks; they could fit anyone.

But that isn't what happened. Instead of looking at my gifts with me, she paused and then gently placed before me the highest bar of life I had experienced to date. "Well, if you want to do what Jesus would do, you could gift the best gift you have."

> She paused and then gently placed before me the highest bar of life I had experienced to date.

That was all she said. No coercion. No convincing. No hovering to see what I would do. She casually walked away, leaving me to choose.

Her words surprised me. I sat stumped and silent. For me, there was only one gift that would qualify as best or even good. The rest were just clothes. Still, I looked through the tops and skirts and tried to imagine which clothing item I could convince myself was the best gift I could give. Down inside, I did want to do what Jesus would do. I just didn't want to give my only fun present. What, oh what should I do? Eventually, I could only conclude that none of the clothes would be my best gift. Only the game would count.

So, the decision remained. Did I want to do what Jesus would do? I didn't have to if I didn't want to. Mom and Dad were not going to make me. Mom had simply advised when asked for input how to do what Jesus would do. Did I? Yes! And no. It was such a painful choice. I pondered and then pushed it all out of my mind until later. The game sat unopened. The box waited at the door, and no one talked about it. Maybe Mom would change her mind. Maybe Mom would forget. After hours passed, I hoped she had reconsidered.

But she hadn't. In fact, after a few hours, she called out to us all that the box was still empty, and we each needed to put something in it. She was going to take it to the neighbors within the hour. My heart was heavy. I had decided to do what Jesus would do. And it didn't feel good at all. In fact, I felt a deep pain. The moment I'd been dreading all day was upon me. I walked to the box and gently put the game in. I had tried to remove the dollar bill, so I could at least get the ten candy bars. But it was going to leave a mark on top of the paper-sealed box top and spoil its brand-new look, so I left it alone. Oh, how much it hurt. I went back to the couch and waited.

After a little while, when the box was filled, I watched as my mother came through and picked it up to carry it out the door. I didn't know, but I was about to receive my best Christmas gift ever.

> A floodgate of joy opened up and burst inside of me, filling my heart with unspeakable delight.

As I watched Mom open the front door and walk across the threshold, my game and the other gifts in tow, a floodgate of joy opened up and burst inside of me, filling my heart with unspeakable delight. It flooded my mind and my entire being! I had never experienced such joy. It was shocking. I couldn't stop smiling for the pleasure of having given away my absolute best to someone who needed it more than I did.

I didn't know it, but I was experiencing something Jesus promised when he said, "Give, and it will be given to you. A good measure, pressed down, shaken together and running over, will be poured into your lap" (Luke 6:38). My mother had had the courage to put before me the painful choice of doing what Jesus would do in a season when it wasn't easy to choose.

But Jesus himself had put it before me, before all of us, long before she did. And he had added a promise. That day, he delivered! As painful as the choice was, so joyful was his return on my gift. When I opened my presents that day, I had thought I would be sad all week. But instead, all week I experienced a brand-new flavor of happiness, a delight that kept coming day after day. And that joy was my best Christmas gift ever.

Looking Back

I wonder what the Osco Drug clerk was thinking as a little tike like me brought such a gem of a booklet up to the cash register with my big happy grin on my face.

On a more serious note, I reflect on what my mom put before me and understand that it would have been perfectly legitimate, and even a gesture of love from a tender mother's heart, had Mom said, "Oh, you've had a hard Christmas and only one toy. Just pick out one of the clothing items you don't want and put that in the box."

But Mom and Dad were people who took the high road. They wanted us to learn what it meant to be one who followed Jesus from the heart. That day, they gave me my first deep experience in trusting the teachings of Christ even when it cost me—and receiving in return a much richer blessing than I could have imagined or they could have anticipated.

I would need the memories of joys like that in the years and decades to come as I made more costly choices to "do what Jesus would do," choices that kept me as a single adult much longer than I anticipated. It isn't that following Jesus leads to a long single adulthood. I have plenty of friends who made the same choices I did but married young as they'd hoped to do. And I know plenty of folks who don't follow Jesus but also remain alone in life when they'd prefer to marry. But for many of us, following Jesus definitely limits the field of available people to date.

One more fun note, although it's more of a looking forward from 1970 way into my future. When my husband learned of this story, he hunted down the game Battling Tops on eBay and gave it to me for Christmas! Forty-some years later, the game came back to me. And I think there was a little rip on the top where a dollar had once been taped. Just kidding!

Two

FREEDOM FOR FIFTEEN?

Age seventeen. God would not leave me alone! And why I heard him so clearly, I can only guess. But I did. It started in the fall of my senior year of high school. A young couple named Tom and Julie, friends of my parents, were starting a Bible study for teens. I was interested in the idea of studying the Bible with other people my age. It didn't hurt that Tom and Julie were young, hip, and fun.

The study started in September of 1978 and eventually grew into a popular place for youth. But in that first year, it was just me, a guy named Mark, and Tom and Julie. Mark was funny and gregarious. He was also gorgeous. A stunning head of feathered blond hair framed his piercing brown eyes, hair that was cut to that seventies length of just far enough below the ears to be curly but not long enough to be shabby. And if Mohawks and mullets had hit the scene by then (fortunately, they hadn't), they would have looked good on him too!

Sometimes I even wonder if I would have been so faithful to attending the Bible study if Mark had been unattractive. I'm fairly sure I would have been less consistent if Mark had been plain. But since he was all that, he was a factor in my commitment to the group because that's what I was about at that time in my life: meeting cute guys.

The Bible study was very laid back. We sat on the floor in a circle, with each of us taking turns to read whatever passage of the Bible we were studying at the time. I found it inspirational to discuss what the Scriptures had to say. Occasionally, I invited friends to join us if I thought God could work on their hearts. But the reality was, God had some work to do in *my* heart. In fact, he had one big thing he was trying to do with me, and it took a good five months for me to let him do it.

> But the reality was, God had some work to do in my heart.

But first, let me share a back story. In the summer of 1970, I had attended a Billy Graham crusade with my parents, held at the McCormick Place in downtown Chicago. As George Beverly Shea began to sing "Just as I Am" at the pinnacle altar call, I eagerly asked my parents if I could respond to the invitation from Reverend Graham to go down to the stage and ask Jesus into my heart.

They were thrilled to hear it, as they had already done so themselves in the last year. Even though they had always celebrated belief in Jesus, asking him into their hearts brought a personal aspect to their relationship with him that included a new joy. And prayer became a two-way street instead of a one-way street as they learned to hear God, to follow his voice. It was different from the approach of just praying and walking away. I can still see their faces as they replied to my request with an enthusiastic, "Of course!" and "Yes!"

I did go down to receive Christ that day. And in the ensuing years, as my parents filled our house with burlap banners of felt letters that proclaimed "Jesus Is Lord!" or "Joy," I was right there with them cutting out the letters with gusto. I joined them for prayer meetings, went on religious retreats, and learned a lot about God. And of course, I even gave away my best Christmas toy to do what Jesus would do.

In high school, I continued to enjoy the spiritual heritage I had received and loved to talk about God. I listened as the after-dinner Bible readings became a regular part of our evening meal. Dad would intersperse explanations of the passages to us and teach us his understanding of who God was and what the Scriptures were saying. It was fun when my brother Mike read because he would put on his best British accent. This was particularly helpful when we got to the long genealogy lists.

But despite all these positives, by my senior year, when I attended Tom and Julie's Bible study, something wasn't right about my spiritual life. I enjoyed hearing all the Bible truths my dad, my mom, and Tom and Julie taught. Still, I wasn't ready to let my life be led by these truths. I wanted my life to be led by me. And as we met for Bible study each week, one thing became noticeably clear. Mark was different in the way his faith affected his life. As he talked about sharing his belief in Jesus with people at school, I thought about how I wasn't doing that so much.

The truth is I was getting drunk with my friends, seeking attention in inappropriate ways, and always, always trying to meet my own needs. Mark was a leader at school and wanted to bring God into his social circle. It was the priority of his life. He came to the study with questions about his faith and how to reach his friends. As I listened to his enthusiastic questions for insight, I felt bad about the way I was living my own life compared to him.

As I privately pondered Mark's life and exposed my heart to the Bible each week, the Holy Spirit began speaking clearly to me about something that I didn't care too much to hear. In fact, God and I had a month-long conversation that went something like this:

> God: Annie, I want you to make a decision to obey me.
>
> Me: Huh?
>
> God: I want you to make a decision to obey me. For the rest of your life.
>
> Me: Are you talking to me?
>
> God: Yes. I want you to make a decision to obey me for the rest of your life.

I was surprised! I hadn't been aware that I didn't have my heart set on obeying God. I had felt rather good about how much I loved God and talked about him with people. But faced with this decision, I realized I didn't want in.

> Me: (girlsplainin' to God how things work) God, you know how you said you want me to make this decision to obey you? Well, I've been thinking about that. I can't do it. I could never keep a commitment like that. I just couldn't. I could try, but . . . it wouldn't be right to make that decision since I won't be able to follow through.
>
> God: Leave that to me.
>
> Me: Say what?
>
> God: That's my responsibility.
>
> Me: What do you mean?
>
> God: Make a decision to obey me and leave to me the responsibility of fulfilling that promise.
>
> Me: But that doesn't make any sense.
>
> God: Trust me.

Me: You want me to make a decision to obey you for the rest of my life. But you say you are going to assume the responsibility of my keeping it?

God: Yes.

Me: But that doesn't make any sense!

God: Trust me.

I spent several weeks trying to put my mind around what God was saying to me but couldn't understand it. I went to school. Did my homework. Hung out with my friends. Ate dinner with my family. Practiced Christmas songs in Concert Choir. Rocked to the Beatles with my partner in Swing Choir. Discoed to new Abba songs with my friends at the community Teen Town Dance. I may have even gotten drunk at a party.

And all the while, constantly and secretly, my mind was drifting, wondering, pondering . . . how was it that God was asking me to make a decision I felt I couldn't keep and telling me to leave the results to him?

I didn't ask anyone about my dilemma. In fact, I wouldn't have told my parents because we didn't have an intimate, conversational relationship where we could talk about something like this. Or perhaps it was because I wanted them to believe my spiritual life was already in good shape.

After trying to figure it out but being unable, one day, I finally just accepted that the concept was beyond my understanding. I had clearly heard what God had said. I knew what I had replied, and I got the gist of his rebuttal. So, I came back to the table.

Me: God, I think I've got what you are saying to me. Well, I don't truly understand it, but I accept it. And since it is you talking, I see it as the right thing to do. And I will do it. I will make a decision to obey you. But I need some time before I do it.

I need—I want—time to run my own life for a while. You see, I'm a senior in high school (I was spelling it out again). I'm ready to go to college and be on my own. My *own*. I've been trying to obey my parents for almost eighteen years, and I just need some time to make my own decisions . . . not be under anyone's thumb . . . be my own boss.

So, how about if I turn eighteen, graduate, and then run my own life for a while. Say for, oh, about fifteen years? And then, when I'm thirty-three, I will make an all-out decision to obey you. You can call the shots after that. Does that sound good? Can I just have freedom for fifteen?

> Out of billions of people in the world, he cares about each one of us personally.

God: There are a few problems with that. First, fifteen years is a long time. You may not be able to come back to me after that long of living on your own. A lot of people put me off until the future. And they get used to running their own lives. They often don't come back.

Me: But God, you know I love you. I just want to make my own decisions for a while.

God: But I can't protect you in that scenario.

Me: But . . .

God: The guidance I offer you is an umbrella—only meant to protect you from the elements of this world.

Me: But . . .

God: When you step outside of my protection, you expose yourself to hurts that are outside of my will for you.

Me: Oh.

God: You could hurt yourself without heeding my guidance.

Me: I could see that.

God: And Annie—

Me: Yes?

God: When you tell me you want to put me off until later, it hurts me.

Me: It hurts you? Little me can hurt *you*?

God: Yes. You are my only you.

I reluctantly heard the things God had said to this point, but the thought that I would matter so much to God that he would hurt because of my distancing him caught my attention. Out of billions of people in the world, he cares about each one of us personally—so much that putting him off would hurt him.

That was the part of the conversation I couldn't get out of my mind. While I thought I could be strong and come back to God later, and while I was hungry to be on my own, I didn't want to be one more person in the world who took God for granted and rejected his guidance. After all, he was my very Creator. Our relationship couldn't get more intimate than that.

After this conversation, I could no longer pretend that God would happily watch me run my life and make my own decisions while shutting him out. Or that he would nod approvingly at all the good things I would do in my own power without even consulting him, let alone relying on him. I mean, what parents raises their children so they can go off and do good things to impress them but never talk to them? It doesn't make sense in an earthly way, so why did I think it made sense in my relationship with God?

I told God I would make the decision to obey him, but I still needed a little time, not fifteen years but a little time to get my will lined up. I meant weeks, but it took me three months and three nudges from the Holy Spirit to finally make the decision. The first two times, I heard the Holy Spirit whisper to me, "What about that decision you plan to make? What about today?"

I would say, with a bit of panic, "No, I'm not ready!"

Finally, one day in February of 1979, early in the morning, as I was about to leave my bedroom and head downstairs for breakfast (it was probably more like a bagel grab and a quick and panicked walk to the bus stop), I heard what seemed to be the Holy Spirit saying, "Annie, you said you were going to make the decision to obey. If you meant it, what keeps you from making the decision in this moment? *Why not now*?"

This time, there was an urgency and a tone of frustration I hadn't sensed before. And the question was more to the point. If I meant it, how could I not do it right now? I realized it was time to let go. I exhaled in resignation, got down on my knees, put my hands in the air, and declared, "Okay, okay! I'll obey you!" And that was the beginning of my commitment to an obedient walk of faith in Jesus.

"Whoever has my commands and keeps them is the one who loves me. The one who loves me will be loved by my Father, and I too will love them and show myself to them." (John 14:21)

Looking Back

When I think of those months, I am amazed at the clarity with which God spoke to me. Over the years, I have found his voice to vacillate between crystal clear and vague. I see that pattern even with his first twelve disciples.

When people say they wish Jesus were here to talk with them face-to-face so they could understand him clearly, I think about the time Jesus warned his disciples to beware the yeast of the Pharisees, and they asked each other if he was mad at them because no one had brought any bread. Whatever the reason, there are times when it is easier to understand God's voice, and there are times when vagueness calls me to keep asking until things become clear. But in those months of my senior high school year, I had the privilege of hearing a truly clear message, a persistent wooing.

I wonder if part of the reason I heard God so clearly at the time was that my mother was regularly fasting and praying every Monday. I know she was concerned for my spirituality because of letters she wrote to my dad at that time as part of a marriage enrichment program they attended (he gave these to me after she died, and nope, I wasn't fooling anyone, it turns out).

So, at least, one of the things she was praying and fasting about was likely my spiritual commitment. I also realize that while I had a lot of emotional love for God at the time, I didn't know Jesus taught that to love God is to obey him.

Bringing this chapter back to the theme of living as a single person who wants to marry, I can't deny that if I had to choose between being married without Jesus and being single with Jesus, I would definitely choose Jesus. I know that I know this because it's basically what I did for most of my life.

In other words, there were always men around that weren't followers of Jesus—whether at work, at a gym, or even at church.

Enough of these guys were interested in me over the years to have found myself in a relationship and on the way down the aisle. But this wasn't worth the cost of leaving behind the vision of a life centered on Jesus.

I know others who made this difficult choice and waited longer than usual to find love and family.* But it was worth it because Jesus is the greatest source of love and acceptance any of us can find—if we press in close to him.

Not too many years ago, I was thinking about the people who are like I was before age seventeen, those looking all the time for love from a human but never for love from their Creator. I wanted to write a song that captured my testimony of being in this state and finally trusting God with my heart.

This song is not in any way meant to say not to look for a spouse or life partner. It's about starting a search for love with God because he truly is the one that took the nail for each of us.

* This is not to say there is a direct correlation. Many married Christians I know found each other at a young age. Devotion does not equal delay. For me, it did in this area but not in other areas. Every follower's life is unique.

Gotta Get My Love in Your Heart

I was dancing round the town
He was whispering
Gotta get my love in your heart
All the boys were being clowns
He was calling
I am your missing part

His love coming down to me
Was the love that took the nail
I was searching for a lover's arms
He turned my heart; he turned my sail

I was losing at my game
He was offering
Come and make a new start
I was shopping for a dream
He kept knocking
Put my love in your cart

His love coming down to me
Was the love that took the nail
I was searching for a lover's arms
He turned my heart; he turned my sail

Now he's got me at his side
He still whispers
You've got my love in my heart
So if you're shopping for a dream
Hear me say he
Might be your missing part

His love coming down to you
Is the love that took the nail
If you're searching for a lover's arms
Let him turn your heart; Let him turn your sail

Three

ONE MOMENT, A FOREVER DECISION

Age nineteen. I just wanted to kiss somebody! Before college, I didn't perceive dating as something that would lead to marriage. Having a boyfriend and someone to kiss was just part of the way I perceived growing in relationship skills. I hoped for a guy that I could give affection to and who could give affection to me.

Most of the four years of high school, I managed to find my way into at least one relationship with a nice but immature guy to match my nice but immature self. I had no discernment of whom I would date, and my parents hadn't taught me much about choosing. Instead, my mom encouraged me to pray for a good husband.

My mother approved of my first boyfriend—even though I was fourteen and he seventeen, and even though I wasn't supposed to date until I was sixteen—because he played guitar at church.

A year later, when my second boyfriend and I broke up, my mom teased me that it wasn't a real break-up because it wasn't a real boyfriend since I hadn't officially reached the age of sixteen. (He should have played guitar at church!) There were a few other guys in subsequent years, but I took all these relationships in stride.

> I had no direction about whom I should date or what sort of guy I wanted to marry.

Once I got to college at the University of Wisconsin-Madison, I expected I might meet someone I would marry. But I still had no direction about whom I should date or what sort of guy I wanted to marry. One day, I talked with a Christian friend as we walked across campus. I told her about a guy that had caught my eye. She gently asked if he was a believer in Jesus. When I said I didn't know, she threw out an idea. "As a Christian, have you thought about only dating Christians?"

This was a new idea to me, but as she described her own decision and her rationale, I got it. If I was going to obey God throughout my life, it didn't make sense to try to do that while married to someone who didn't share that value. And since dating can lead to love and marriage and a baby carriage, why not guard my heart for Jesus and limit dating to those that followed him? So, instead of taking months to decide, this time, I made the decision on the spot. Sure, I'll limit myself to dating Christians. That makes sense. And hey, there were a lot of Christian men around campus.

Looking Back

When I made the decision that day, I didn't know I wouldn't develop any romantic relationships in college, despite all those available men. It isn't that no one ever asked me out. I went on dates. I'll never forget the summer after my freshman year when four different guys from separate social circles asked me out for the same night!

Can you believe I stayed home? Maybe decisions like that one are why a long-term relationship never happened in college! Seriously though, there were people interested, but none of them felt like the right guy for me. And the ones I *was* interested in didn't have the same draw to me.

I also didn't know when I made that decision, I wouldn't meet my husband until ten years later or that I wouldn't marry him for even longer. IEven so, it was an easy and right decision to make.

Four

WAS GOD CALLING ME TO BE SINGLE?

Age twenty. The doubt wouldn't go away. It's difficult, even now, to assess and understand the reason why, in my junior year of college, I struggled to believe I would marry. When I arrived at college, I'd had a full expectation to hitch up with a good guy. And I seemed to have an easy time believing for God's provision in other areas. I had learned to apply the principle Jesus taught—about putting first the kingdom of God, and he would take care of the rest—in school, friendships, finances, and finding a job.

In fact, I *knew* graduating from college that God was going to put a job into my lap. I had absolute confidence and no fear. But before then, halfway through college, I began to struggle to believe he would do the same for me in marriage.

The doubt started circa 1981 when I was listening to a talk for young adults, surrounded by one or two hundred others, mostly in our twenties. An older student spoke on the apostle Paul's comments regarding marriage and singleness from 1 Corinthians chapter 7. This is a chapter in the Bible where Paul writes to some Christians at a church in Corinth to answer questions they had about the choice of staying single.

The speaker said something that, for some reason, planted a fear that I would remain single all my days, even though, like most others, I wanted the family life I'd grown up with. First, he explained Paul's argument for remaining single to better serve God.

From Paul's perspective, marriage was less of a source of support and encouragement for serving God and more of a distraction from the work to be done for the kingdom. "An unmarried woman or virgin is concerned about the Lord's affairs: Her aim is to be devoted to the Lord in both body and spirit. But a married woman is concerned about the affairs of this world—how she can please her husband" (1 Corinthians 7:34).

> I feared that God would choose a life of aloneness for me because he knew I wanted to serve him wholeheartedly.

The student presented Paul's ideas about this, perhaps as the main thrust of his talk. Then he said the words, "God probably wants some of you to remain single." Hearing this, after the emphasis on the idea that singleness was better for serving God, put a message in my heart that marriage would be a compromise to serving God with all my heart.

I feared that God would choose a life of aloneness for me because he knew I wanted to serve him wholeheartedly. This fear would remain with me until I was old enough and mature enough to understand the passage better, in the context of the whole chapter.

Here is what I now understand. First, Paul makes it clear he is only sharing his *opinion*, "I have no command from the Lord, but I give a judgment as one who by the Lord's mercy is trustworthy (v. 25)."

Second, I realized over time that the Bible presents a whole picture that marriage is God's provision and design for an abundant life and even for serving him. It's his answer for loneliness according to Genesis 2:18: "The LORD God said, 'It is not good for the man to be alone. I will make a helper suitable for him.'" Also, Paul recognizes that it's God's avenue for fulfillment of the sex drive when he writes, "But since sexual immorality is occurring, each man should have sexual relations with his own wife, and each woman with her own husband" (1 Corinthians 7:2).

Third, Paul argues in this chapter for people to *choose* to live the Christian life single, just as Paul himself has. He's not asking people to figure out if God is calling them to be single. And nowhere does Paul call marriage a compromise.

Fourth, over time, it also became clear to me through other speakers on this passage that Paul was most likely responding to an inquiry from people in Corinth looking for support for staying single. They may have been looking for too much support, as in they may have felt that no one should marry. The evidence of this is that Paul goes out of his way to also defend marriage. This insight made a big difference to me.

Fifth, I discovered in reading carefully through the chapter that Paul concludes with three *requirements* for anyone who *wants* to live a single life. Singleness is tough, and it requires some grit. And these requirements draw quite a different picture than a message that God has destined some people for singleness. Anyone wondering if God is calling them to a life of singleness can assess themselves for these three marks: "But the man who [1] has settled the matter in his own mind, [2] who is under no compulsion but [3] has control over his own will, and who has made up his mind not to marry the virgin—this man also does the right thing" (v. 37). Paul makes it clear that a decision not to marry is very personal and requires a person to settle it completely on their own will. No spiritual leader is to place such a burden on another person.

Yet, for some reason, a lot of married, everyday spiritual leaders put emphasis on the "better single" messages of this passage instead of the side of the coin that says, "You want to be single? Here's how to prove you can do it!" But I honestly can't remember hearing a pastor who was *single* encourage people to consider being single for the sake of serving God.

Sometimes, church leaders teach 1 Corinthians 7 to the unmarried to emphasize singleness as a superior way to serve God even while it teaches the full congregation that marriage is the foundation of the church. Has anyone else been thrown off by hearing both of these messages from the same body?

It probably happens, but very few pastors are single unless they're a youth pastor (and when they are, everyone but everyone is trying to marry them off!). I've never seen a ministry, other than a single adult ministry, run entirely, or even mostly, by single people. In my experience, most pastors, most people in other full-time ministry roles, and most volunteers are married.

In other words, when I looked around at ministry co-leaders, whether I served for high school youth, children's ministry, worship team, or any type of ministry, usually more than or at least half of the leaders were married. And everyone on the team was giving up time to serve.

So, it's difficult to see the evidence that singleness in current times and current cultures opens us up to serve more. If singleness were superior for serving God, wouldn't we find it most prevalent among those dedicated to full-time ministry?

Finally, over time, I observed that Paul's assertion that a single person is more strongly focused on the Lord's concerns didn't seem to apply to me as a single adult extrovert living in America. I spent much time in my twenties, thirties, and forties arranging get-togethers to meet needs for emotional connection—both my own and those of others. This took a lot of time and effort!

Even daily, when living alone, I had to spend a lot of effort finding outlets to talk about my day with close friends on the phone. Who was available to talk? Okay, I talked to her yesterday, who can I talk to today? Now that I'm married, it happens naturally. Or I simply have companionship knowing my husband is rattling around somewhere in the house. I need to invest much less effort into meeting my social needs as a married person.

The apostle Paul loved being single or at least believed in it wholeheartedly for the freedom it brought him to focus on the kingdom of God. He supported and encouraged the choice for others but gave grave warnings that it wasn't a decision or a choice to be made lightly and that only those who could control themselves should attempt it. Jesus agreed. When speaking on choosing the single life, he taught, "Not everyone can accept this word, but only those to whom it has been given (Matthew 19:11).

Neither Paul nor Jesus said God's choice of singleness for people would be revealed by a lack of finding a life partner. Nor is the choice given to an unwilling heart. Rather, if God gives the choice of singleness to someone, they will know it because they will be able to accept it. I venture they would *want* it! And for those who do, more power to them for the advantages they want and experience. However, anyone who dislikes the idea of being single but has worked to accept it out of a sense of compulsion or guilt should let themselves off the hook! That is exactly what I came to do as I matured in Christ and grew in my understanding of 1 Corinthians 7.

I wish that anyone who preaches "God will select some of you to be single" would change their message to something more aligned with Paul's and Christ's teaching. For example, "Some of you might find yourself wanting to be single. If you do, make sure you meet the criteria listed by Paul in 1 Corinthians 7:37: you've made up your own mind, there's no compulsion, and you have control over your own will."

Looking Back

I think of conversations I had with various people that seemed intended to deter me from wanting marriage. It's hard to put my mind around why they wanted to steer my thoughts away from my desire. For example, when, in my mid-thirties, I explained to a friend/mentor how lonely I was. He told me to look out on the crowd around us and realize how the people I saw were doubly burdened with their own issues and the issues of their spouses.

Inside I was thinking, "Huh. What happened to the doubled blessings and divided hurts adage that most people promote of what marriage can be?"

It turned out the latter was likely what this friend actually believed. At his daughter's wedding a year later, he publicly described how he had prayed daily for a spouse for her. Clearly, he wasn't aiming to double her burdens through his prayers.

So, why did he feel he had to present a burdensome picture of marriage to comfort me in my loneliness? And a picture that wasn't a true reflection of what was in his heart? When the truth came out, it was very strange to think about what he had said to me that day. Instead of trying to reason me out of desiring a family, I wish he had just lifted my heart and its desires and its loneliness up to Jesus.

Five

LET IT SNOW

Age twenty-four. Have you ever had a vision from God? After college, I landed a job teaching high school French and English in a small Wisconsin town called Mosinee. Friends helped me find an apartment and roommate in nearby Stevens Point, and I began my life as a professional. I was a bit sad to be moving away from the church I loved and the friends I knew so well—so much that I would drive back to Madison nearly every other weekend in my first year of teaching. But over time, I adapted to my life in Stevens Point and spent more time there with new friends. I found a solid church where I continued to grow in my faith and experienced the joys and challenges that come with the early years of teaching.

In 1985, after my first year, I took a typical Wisconsin summertime job of working on a farm. I picked cucumbers, but I especially enjoyed building a relationship with the farmers and spoiling the snow-white calves with way too much petting. In the fall, I had the joy of seeing the farm owners, Donna and then Jeff, come to Christ through the working of the Holy Spirit. Then came the joy of discipling Donna and another new believer at our church. What a wonderful year that was—one of those times when God was stirring and bringing growth. In fact, that year, he did something else for me that would apply to many years to come.

After reading Christian biographies, I began asking God to give me a calling.

> After reading Christian biographies, I began asking God to give me a calling.

One evening, I lay down on my bed and continued my prayer for that season, "God, please give me a mission!" But before I fell asleep that night, almost as soon as I lay my head on the pillow, I found myself in a vision. I call it a vision because it was vividly clear—in color (most dreams are black and white)—and specific things happened in a logical order. In the secular world, this is called a lucid dream. But as a believer, I trust the Bible's promise that God speaks to us in visions and dreams and differentiates a regular dream from a vision through this lucidity.

I'd had a couple of visions in the past. The meaning of the first was revealed to me as soon as it ended. The second was revealed four days later as I attended a class for college-age adults. For that vision, as the message was delivered, the meaning of the vision was suddenly clear, and I knew it was for the whole group of us, not just for me. So, I shared it with the group, and it was well-received. I won't digress into those visions. Suffice it to say, they meaningfully spoke to others and me, were revealed in unique timing for each, and boosted my confidence in God's speaking to me through visions.

So, in the summer of eighty-five, as I experienced a vision from God, I recognized it and knew God would reveal its meaning. In this vision, I found myself in the driver's seat of my orange Pinto wagon—a car that many mocked but my mechanics loved. I was traveling in northern Wisconsin on a county highway that passed through a forest.

It was a bright sunny day. It wasn't snowing, but there was snow piled up everywhere, with three or four inches of snow on the road and a set of tire tracks clearly visible along the way in front of me. In the vision, I knew my mission was to follow those tracks wherever they led. At first, they were heading due west.

As I approached a three-way intersection at which I could only go straight or take a right-hand turn, the tire tracks I was following turned to the north, and I went that way. As I rounded the corner, the road was closely lined with beautiful, full eighty-foot-tall evergreen trees. There was no other car in sight at any point in the vision. The road going north had a rise about a hundred feet ahead, a hill I could not see past. But even though it was a bright sunny day, I could see the light from a city shining beyond the hill. Yes, the light coming from the city outshined the sunlight!

As I drove about forty feet farther, the road ahead was suddenly three feet deep in snow. And yet, I knew my mission was to get up and over that hill. I got out of my car and thought for a moment about shoveling my way down the road, only to immediately hear myself say aloud, "I'm going to need a shovel to get my car out of the way for the snowplow." Somehow, I knew a snowplow would come out of the woods and onto the road I was on. I knew I'd hop on the plow with the driver to push forward toward the city through the three-foot snow.

As soon as I declared my need for a shovel, I had a bright red plastic shovel in my hands. As I moved toward the shoulder to begin making a place for my car, I heard myself say, "I'm going to need a pair of gloves to protect my hands from the work." And just like that, I had a pair of gloves on my hands. But they weren't work gloves or outdoor snow gloves. They were bright shimmery satiny white gloves with sequin embellishments. On the inside of my hand, they stopped before my wrist and had a small pearl button and loop closure, allowing them to fit very snugly.

I looked at them in astonishment and asked, "What kind of gloves are these?!"

A voice from above replied, "They're wedding gloves."

I exclaimed, "Wedding gloves?! These aren't the right gloves for the job."

This time, the voice replied inaudibly to my heart and refuted me, "*Yes they are. Look again.*" I did so and saw that the gloves' beauty gave me joy and strength.

I declared aloud, "These *are* the right gloves for the job!" I then approached the snow to begin making a place to put my car on the shoulder of the road.

But before I could start, a small, somewhat dirty, and vicious West Highland terrier came out of nowhere, snarling and lunging toward me to attack me. I thought, "This is sad, but I'm going to have to use the shovel to kill the dog." I raised my shovel to bring it down on the dog, and while I looked up at the red shovel, the dog squealed and went running off toward the direction of the city of light.

And at that, the vision ended.

> The meaning of the vision came to me over many years as various things played out in my life.

I was wide awake and sat up, asking God what the vision meant. Well, a divine explanation did not come when the vision ended. And it didn't come four days later either, not even in the months to come. The meaning of the vision came to me over many years as various things played out in my life. At the time, there were hints but also obscurity.

For example, over a few months, as I shared the vision with others, several believers opined that snow in a vision from God had to do with purity and suggested that my work to move snow might indicate God was calling me to a work involving sexual purity. Others declared that the wedding gloves and the call to look at them again surely meant I would marry one day.

I talked about the vision with a pastor back in Madison, who understood and had experienced that God doesn't necessarily reveal the meaning of some visions until they are realized—perhaps years later! He shared a vision the Lord had given him when he was younger. The Lord had someone draw for him a pole with four poles coming off of it.

Much later, the vision unfolded, and its meaning revealed that it represented four young men who he trained as leaders years after he had received the drawing. He shared how he understood what the vision meant only when it came to pass. He suggested the Lord would do the same with me and recommended I avoid interpreting what it meant beforehand—that visions and prophecies are often better appreciated for confirming events when they happen rather than predicting things.

This approach to waiting proved to be fruitful. Eventually, the meaning of the vision became clear as my life unfolded, and portions of the vision happened.

I held from the beginning that the evergreen trees lining the path in my vision represented the truth of the gospel (they point to heaven and are ever *green*) that surrounds every day of our lives.

The hill in the road represented my short little life as I travel toward the city of light, so bright that it outshines the brilliant sun in the sky! (Sorry, Paris, as much as I love you, *this* city of light was heaven, not you!)

A major part of the vision, the snow, did turn out to be related to something several friends pondered—purity. It hinted ten years into the future at the education programs I'd manage to help young people delay sexual activity.

It made sense that the bright red shovel represented the blood of Christ, shed to overcome the sinful temptations of life represented in the off-white and vicious West Highland terrier (terriers everywhere, you know I love you).

And the gloves—the *wedding* gloves—hinted at the marriage that would come even further in the future. God cared enough about my earnest prayers at age twenty-four to give me some hints about a love to come, even though we wouldn't date until many years later. And it even reflected on the experience I needed to go through to "look again" at marriage to see its value and to end the temptation to see it as a compromise.

As for the snowplow, I am still working out its meaning.

God gave visions like mine to characters in the Bible and to other believers I know too. I hope for others in need of encouragement or direction to experience this same profound experience.

Looking Back

My work in abstinence education started when I was thirty-three years old. That was the age where seventeen-year-old me thought it would be a good time to suddenly begin obeying God with my life. How would I possibly have been prepared to lead a Christian ministry?

Six

THE CHALLENGE

WARNING: This chapter is whiney. While it ends on a high note, the bulk of it is meant to recognize some of the difficulties of marrying later than expected and to give some readers an opportunity to feel as though their "left behind" feelings are valid, that someone understands. Not everyone experiences extended singleness the way I did. But I'm sharing candidly for those that do.

Age twenty-six. Friends were disappearing into the married vortex! In my late twenties, I was back in Madison, Wisconsin, after having taught in Mosinee, Wisconsin for two years and then in West Africa as a missionary teacher for one year. I had intended to stay in Dakar, Senegal, for three years, but it turned out that teaching middle school wasn't my thing. So, back to the United States I went to find a teaching job with high schoolers again. I started my search back in the town of my alma mater and landed a job in Madison.

I was reestablishing old friendships and meeting new friends. When I had left Madison three years previously, most of my friends were graduating from college, and a few were getting married. But by now, there were many more who had tied the knot and were creating families. I spent time with friends in the married universe—the one I wanted to be in—and I spent time in the single universe—the one where most of us had meaningful lives but wanted to graduate into the other universe. Since infancy, we'd been raised to understand that marriage would be a natural progression of life, and we were searching for someone to share life with.

And yet, in the mid to late twenties, finding that *someone* evaded many of us. Spending time with friends in the married universe could be taunting: Do you see how happy this universe is? The people over here have found someone to love, as they expected. They are done with the dating game and are building their families. They're having kids! Isn't that what you expected too? Why can't you find someone?

> The challenge of having to reestablish new friends who were single and available became a repeating cycle.

As available Christian men disappeared into the married vortex, and as married friends had diminished availability, the challenge of having to reestablish new friends who were single and available became a repeating cycle. I could be six months into a new friendship, establishing true trust and camaraderie, and the friend would begin dating, marry, and, at least for a while, disappear.

And if they came back, their time was limited. They were no longer available for weekend travel—except maybe for a group campout weekend. Male friends were only available as less-than-intimate friends, as they rightly sought to honor their relationships with their wives. They would certainly never again be available for a long tête-à-tête conversation that provided male companionship and insights.* Others shared this same frustration with me. One person even described the repeated loss of close friends as serial divorce.

Friendships didn't always end or change in these ways. Some married friends were still available and easy to relate to, and some singles remained single. But I learned that friendships were always capable of changing at any time in the way described, and so they felt more precarious than when I was in college. I discontinued the habit of spending most of my time with one best friend and diversified to survive the risk of continued loss.

When I talked to friends about being lonely as a single, if they had married young, it was difficult for some to understand how single life changes as one progresses from early to late twenties. They looked back on their single years as a time of fun and joy and fellowship. They remembered the parties, the laughter, the pranks, the retreats, the enthusiasm!

They imagined that my life in my late twenties held the same quality as their twenty-two-year-old single lifestyle had held. Some friends even refuted any description of feeling lonely as a single person, contradicting my feelings with glowing descriptions of what fun they had when single. They seemed set in a belief that the good times couldn't possibly fade for single adults.

But these hadn't experienced what it meant to feel "left behind" as others married. Some went from living with college roommates to living with their spouse. They never had even a year of coming home to an empty house.

---

* I even experienced this with my brothers and with my father when he remarried after my mother's death. And I would venture that some of my and my husband's relatives and friends experienced some of this after we married and became less available.

Honestly, I could have my house *filled* with forty people attending a party and then feel lonely as soon as the last person walked out the door! There was no one with whom to process the night, rejoice, or return the house to its normal state and clean up the dishes.

Anyone can make assumptions that busy, healthy people are not lonely. One friend told me a couple of times during my single years how full my life was, even that it was complete. It baffled me when she said these words because they seemed to imply that it was impossible for me to feel lonely due to life's fullness. But there came a time when her husband and children were gone for a week. She was home alone, waking, eating meals, and going to bed by herself. She had a taste for seven days of what life was like in an empty house, and she didn't like it! She went out of her way to tell me that she better understood the loneliness I had described.

I'm glad this friend came to recognize what I'd been sharing, but I understand why she'd been telling me how full and complete my life was. When a single adult is out and about and going to gatherings with others, laughing and having fun, or at work in a meaningful job, in those moments, the aloneness that exists back at home is invisible to others. Life looks full. Indeed, it is full. But that doesn't mean it isn't lonely. In some cases, the fuller someone's life is, the more they wish they could share it with a significant other.

And then there are the holidays! Someone I know told her married-with-children brother that she missed opening presents with him and their other siblings on Christmas morning. In response, he reminded her that when they were kids, they opened presents at home and later in the day got together with extended family. The person was so surprised to be called extended family by her brother as he resisted her subtle request to join his family for Christmas. It is understandable that parents want to have a special time with their own children. But if someone gets married and leaves the birth family for a new family, it would be easier on single siblings if the married siblings understood that the single still considers their siblings as their main family. If the married sibling does understand, it doesn't make them responsible for their sibling's happiness. But more empathy than less would be appreciated.

Another challenge for singles is missing the children they wanted to fill their homes and lives. They made their lists of potential names and envisioned how they would be spaced out. They pictured the traditions they would add at home and what they would keep from their own upbringing. But as time goes on, the dream of having children or of raising children side by side with their friends and siblings becomes threatened.

I suppose some people settle and marry someone who doesn't quite feel right so they can get on with the business of having a family. But for the stubborn of heart who wait for a true love, the issue of childlessness can grow with each year. And let's not even get started on all of the baby showers (and bridal showers) that childless women lovingly and enthusiastically attend. No one sees the tears they save for their car ride home.

> "If two lie down together, they will keep warm. But how can one keep warm alone?" (Ecclesiastes 4:11)

It's such a silent pain. When a married mother of two loses a third child in pregnancy, the whole church mourns with her. But no one is going to add to the church prayer list that single person X is now older and hurting for the loss of children they aren't having. And no one would want a reaction quite that strong! But the fact remains that being single and childless is a challenge that can feel invisible.

The Bible recognizes and calls out various challenges of living life alone: "Two are better than one, because they have a good return for their labor: If either of them falls down, one can help the other up. But pity anyone who falls and has no one to help them up. Also, if two lie down together, they will keep warm. But how can one keep warm alone? Though one may be overpowered, two can defend themselves" (Ecclesiastes 4:9–12). As my single adult status continued in my twenties, I related to this passage increasingly.

Waiting long for true love to find its way to my heart was even more difficult in those times when I was unattracted to someone attracted to me. There was a time or two that I tried to make myself like someone who liked me, but it just can't be forced. Well-meaning friends can get frustrated when their matchmaking efforts go unrewarded. But if it doesn't fit, it just doesn't fit!

Finding love is tough! Along the way, I discovered the importance of continuing to ask God for his help. Burying my heart to escape the disappointments or to "stop bothering God" *again* with my unfulfilled hope for a man proved to be a bitter solution. Over time, I realized the best way to face the challenge. Just. Keep. Bringing. My. Loneliness. To. God. Fact is, I once described to a pastor friend named Tom what a struggle the whole thing was. He encouraged me in replying, "But Annie! You are commendable for remaining in the struggle. Do you know how many just quit?"

Also, a message from a wise pastor named Chris really encouraged me to face the challenge. He compared life on Earth to a salmon swimming upstream. So much of it is an effort—a *constant* effort. But as we swim, he said, we pray for God's help in finding the right path and then look for the openings he shows us. I liked that! It applies to anyone's anytime challenge.

True, for some people love comes early, and they escape the many lonely years on the path to love. What a blessing! But for many of us, it's the salmon struggle. And over time, I learned how to pray and find those pathways. I had a long stream to swim, but that also meant I had that many more experiences of God opening up the next passageway on my long swim to find love.

Looking Back

I wish my husband and I could have married at least ten years sooner. Yet, I feel so called to write this book that I hope and pray the long wait will have all been worth the path that led to my sharing my experiences with others. If I can encourage someone with the insights I've gained, more power to the redemption of pain.

Seven

SUPERSTITION

Age twenty-eight. Why can't I find someone?! This question became a drumbeat in the back of my mind as I continued to experience friendships grow faint as besties moved on to marriage. The question still beats for older singles throughout the world today. For me, it led to many conversations with friends in both universes about the *why* question. And since married people had successfully transitioned into the desired universe, their stories had some clout—they had done something right (hopefully). But a theme among many married friends' answers to the question of "why can't I find someone" was this: once they were content being single, God brought them a spouse.

Many encouraged me to become content being single for the purpose of God bringing me a husband. This idea had become a theme in more than one circle of the Christian church where I was living out my early Christian life. I'm not sure if the thought is still out there as strongly as it was when I was a young adult, but I describe in a later chapter how a Christian therapist in 2008 said it was alive and well among her colleagues. So, I wonder if some today still grapple with it. It's an idea that can even be presented as biblical truth.

If only a Christian Snopes type of website had existed for me to check out this strange message. Like a typical Snopes-identified fallacy, it had a lot of forms. They went something like these (and all of these were said to me at one time or another):

"Before I met my spouse, I went through a time of becoming content as a single. *Then* God brought me my spouse."

"When you become content being single, that is when God will bring you a spouse."

"God won't bring you a spouse until you are content being single."

Over time, I came to see this concept as something that wasn't supported by Scripture, and I have even realized that it fits the definition of *superstition*: "a widely held but unjustified belief in supernatural causation leading to certain consequences of an action or event, or a practice based on such a belief."* I consider this a superstition and not a promise from God for several reasons.

For one thing, it isn't written in Scripture anywhere. Nowhere does the Bible state that to find a spouse, you need to first become content without one. The truth is that God describes how he created marriage as a gift for us. Also, he commands us to bring our requests and desires before him. For example, in Philippians 4:6, we read, "Do not be anxious about anything, but in every situation, by prayer and petition, with thanksgiving, present your requests to God."

And how about this beautiful admonition is Psalm 62:8: "Trust in him at all times, you people; pour out your hearts to him, for God is our refuge." And yet, I did the opposite of

---

* Lexico.com, s.v. "superstition," accessed December 8, 2021, https://www.lexico.com/en/definition/superstition.

pouring out my heart to God or asking God for the good gift of marriage because I believed the superstition. Instead, I prayed to be content going through life alone to *cause* God to bring me a life of *not* going through life alone. Isn't that twisted? But it was what people were claiming was the way.

This approach of trying to be content as a single to *manipulate God* to give me a husband was really tricky. How does someone demonstrate they are content? Praying for a spouse would certainly not prove I was content alone. What about thinking about marriage someday or going to a wedding and daydreaming about my own wedding design?

Did I slip up?

Am I content enough?

How does God measure it?

Whoops! I just stared at a wedding dress in a shop window! I'm in trouble now.

> Imagine what life in the church would be like if people were taught the principle of proving contentment to God to receive his blessings for other areas of life.

You might say I was experiencing the torment expressed in the book of Ephesians when we follow a teaching that isn't from God. I was "tossed back and forth by the waves, and blown here and there by every wind of teaching" (Ephesians 4:14).

Imagine what life in the church would be like if people were taught the principle of proving contentment to God to receive his blessings for other areas of life. "Friend, you need to be content without a job before pursuing and preparing for a job." Or how about that we need to be content with no friends before developing friendships, with no education before enrolling in college, with no children before developing a family, with no ministry before developing an outreach.

Or if we apply the contentment superstition to basic human needs, would we teach people to be content thirsty before taking a drink? To be content cold before putting on a sweater? Or to be content with a famished hunger before taking the time to eat? I speak as if a fool to demonstrate that it doesn't make any more sense that God would require that a single adult first be content without human companionship before he would provide a partner. In fact, the book of Genesis tells of God observing that it wasn't good for Adam to be alone and shows his creativity, *determination*, and effort to make a suitable partner for him.

To be sure, contentment is a good thing for all people in all circumstances, and the pursuit of it cannot hurt. But to imply that the gift of marriage only comes after someone is content being single? This attaches a requirement to single adults that complicates their ability to pray, adding frustration to the drumbeat. It stops someone from praying honestly and tempts a single adult to play a game of manipulation with God.

> There I was in my twenties, falling hook, line, and sinker for the idea that I had to prove to God I was content being alone so he would bring me a companion to share life with.

And yet, there I was in my twenties, falling hook, line, and sinker for the idea that I had to prove to God I was content being alone so he would bring me a companion to share life with. I heard it so often!

As I could, I set my heart to be satisfied alone, to pray for contentment as a single adult. But it's a strange phenomenon to pray for what is not in your heart. It's bizarre to pray about something important to you by praying what you think God wants to hear instead of pouring out your heart. It was horrible to fall into the grip of this superstition because when you can't pour out your heart, you risk the seeds and root and growth of bitterness.

Scripture tells us to pour out our hearts to God, to bring him our requests. And the Bible makes it clear that marriage is God's answer to loneliness and the sex drive. So, should a single person be burdened to try to prove they can be single and content so God will send them a partner? That's crazy, isn't it?

Jesus often compared the Father's love with a human's parental love. For example, when he asked, "Which of you, if your son asks for bread, will give him a stone? Or if he asks for a fish, will give him a snake? If you, then, though you are evil, know how to give good gifts to your children, how much more will your Father in heaven give good gifts to those who ask him!" (Matthew 7:9-11). I have a similar question. Would a parent who bought a wonderful birthday present for their child withhold the gift on the child's birthday until the child was content with not getting any birthday presents? That isn't the nature of parenting, and I don't believe it's the nature of our heavenly Father's love toward us.

After years of trying to prove to my maker that I was somewhere that he wasn't asking me to be, I grew honest in my prayers about marriage and singleness. I stopped trying to pray something that wasn't in my heart. I remember where I was the first time I honestly cried out to God in my frustration and poured out my heart about my hope for marriage. And as I describe in the next chapter, wow, he was ready to meet me there in my prayer of truth.

Looking Back

It's a bit sad that believers in Jesus are ready to believe super-stitions. A married but infertile friend told me that there is a set of superstitions for infertile couples too. Some sad samples are "Relax and stop trying, and it will happen" and "Have you prayed about it? If you believed in God, you could get pregnant, no problem."

Instead of offering empty platitudes, let's hold each other in our pains and ask how we can pray. To discover what the person would find encouraging from us to alleviate their pain. And let's contest every superstition that is offered as the answer to life's challenges.

Eight

POURING OUT
MY HEART

Age twenty-eight. I'd been trying to prove to God I was content being single, and it was time to come clean. One evening after dinner in 1989, I turned into the parking lot of the Christian school where I taught, still in Madison, Wisconsin. I was headed toward my classroom for some evening prep for the next day. Maybe it was the effect of entering the big empty school while imagining others at home with their families, but I felt alone in the world and wondered whether I would forever live my life without a family.

I was twenty-eight years old and still young enough to experience a vibrant Christian single community of friends. But single life had grown unsettling after several years of close friends finding love, becoming engaged, marrying, and separating from their single life to attach to their new and forever best friend. Other friends moved away to follow a dream job. It was an experience of serial loss, as I described earlier.

Many of us in our late twenties, surprised we hadn't yet met and married the love of our lives, were hoping to tie a matrimonial knot by the age of thirty. There is a well-worn saying that age is just a number, but I've known a lot of people who had a difficult time approaching age thirty with a null love life, and I was in the throes of it. And besides, in those years, I wanted to raise a dozen kids. Time was running out! But up until this time, I had never asked God about his thoughts on me and children. In fact, I hadn't asked him to talk to me about marriage either. I was busy trying to prove I was content being all alone.

> I felt alone in the world and wondered whether I would forever live my life without a family.

I recall contemplating there in my car how God had answered my questions in the past. It was time to get real with God. In tears and frustration, I told him how lonely I was and asked him to tell me straight out if marriage were in store for me, and if not, could he please just tell me if I was going to be single all my life.

I genuinely believe the Holy Spirit prompted this onslaught of tears and pouring out of my heart at that time and in that space because he wanted to speak to my pain, and he had chosen that evening.

I wiped my tears as I left my car and headed for my classroom to grade papers. But inside the school, waiting for me, was a divine appointment.

Carla, a close friend, was in the lobby, looking for a meeting that turned out to be in a different building. She saw my distraught face and came with me to my classroom to talk out whatever was bothering me. I poured out my heart, all the pain, the questions, and the loud ticking of my biological clock! And then we took it to God.

As we brought this burden to Jesus, Carla sensed God lay three messages on her heart for me: (1) know I was a beautiful person and not to let the waiting period discourage me or cause doubts about who I was, (2) God did have a good man and marriage for me in the future, and (3) the waiting had to do with a spiritual issue that had to be resolved. (I never came to know what the spiritual issue was, and I'm okay with that.)

It was flabbergasting to realize God had these things to say, had led Carla to be in the wrong but right place at the right time, and had stirred up my honest thoughts and questions so much that they spilled out of me into his lap right before I ran into Carla. For the first time, I stopped trying to play a game of manipulation with God. For the first time, I poured out my heart, and he was right there waiting with a loving response. How does he do these things?!

I left this divine appointment encouraged. Even though the encounter with God via Carla didn't get me into the arms of my loved one by age thirty, and I could still find myself doubting over the ensuing years if I would ever find a man, God continued to lead me in a lifelong pattern of bringing him my utmost desires and pouring out my heart. As I did, he was there again and again to listen. He consistently gave

"Trust in him at all times, you people; pour out your hearts to him, for God is our refuge." (Psalm 62:8)

me the same promise. I found my heart growing to believe him, despite the long wait. Episodes like my meeting with Carla, when God spoke right to the core of my current situation, are

some of the most precious memories of my life. God can and has spoken to his followers throughout time. And why wouldn't he speak to me? Or to anyone? He is the God who does not change.

Looking Back

I don't believe the habit of laying my heart's desire out before the Lord made my husband come any earlier than he was meant to come, as there turned out to be a practical reason (and apparently an unknown spiritual reason) we had to wait. But as I learned to go to God with my pain, he would speak to me about my hurting heart, give me promises about the future, and redirect my heart to my present life. I would come out of the prayer energized for the future and more enthusiastic for the life at hand. It's regrettable that I spent many years in a misguided effort to prove to God that I was content, refusing to practice this helpful prayer exercise.

P.S. Little did I know as I prayed with Carla that evening that within a few months, I would meet my husband. And boy oh boy, did I ever like him as a person! But I couldn't possibly have seen him as my future husband at the time. There was a significant barrier between us.

Nine

SPECIAL GUY FRIENDS

Age twenty-eight. Waiting forever to start a family was the last thing I wanted. But as I prayed over my life, asking God for marriage and children, over some time, I seemed to hear him saying two things to my heart. One, I would marry one day but two, I shouldn't depend on a guy to come along and take care of me. I wondered what this meant. Don't daydream about meeting and marrying someone with a big-paying job so I could be a full-time mom? Don't expect love to come too quickly? I wasn't sure, but the thought seemed to have come in, sat down, and made itself comfortable.

It wasn't the worst thought to have. It at least supported an attitude of maturity and adulthood as far as taking care of my life. And at worst, it was a word to the wise to adjust to living alone for the time being.

But I wanted more clarity. I was nearing the milestone age of thirty, and I desired to marry and start a family sooner rather than later. So, I prayed to God, "Lord, if you are telling me I won't marry for a *long* time, could you at least send me close guy friends to bring male input into my life and to bring some degree of male companionship?"

About a month later, I was disappointed when the Lord replied. To be completely honest, he said something I didn't want to hear at all. It happened at a prayer meeting I was hosting. At someone's request, I'd invited a somewhat well-known pastor who was passing through the area to come and to share his heart. It turned out that, like Carla, he had a spiritual gift along the lines of 1 Corinthians 12:8: "To one there is given through the Spirit a message of wisdom, to another a message of knowledge by means of the same Spirit."

He asked if he could go around the room and pray for each person and see if God would say anything to them. We all agreed to this.

> "Lord, if you are telling me I won't marry for a long time, could you at least send me close guy friends?"

When he prayed for me, God gave him a vision and a message related to a ministry project I was involved with. But then he added a postscript: "And God has heard your prayer and is going to be adding friendships to your life."

On the one hand, it's always gratifying to receive a third-party response from someone who knows nothing about me or my private prayers as a confirmation that God has heard me and is answering. It's even a wow moment! But in this situation, it carried an insinuation that I'd continue living my life alone "for a long time." And that was painful to hear.

But alas, I did go on to be single for a long time—and God did bring those friendships with guys along (I had and have a lot of incredible female friends too). In a short time, I started spending a lot of time with my two friends Jerry and Brian (I'll call him Brian #1 because, as you'll soon see, I have a habit of finding friends with identical names). We did a lot together over a period of years. We had a wonderful regular habit of driving out to our church for an early prayer meeting almost daily and coming back to Jerry's apartment to make the best grilled tuna, tomato, pepper sandwiches I remember. Brian heard so many stories about my dad that he learned to imitate some of his behaviors. And he was always ready and willing to work on my car for me, whether changing the oil or the brakes.

Eventually, Brian and Jerry each married and were less available, and while the loss of those friendships are examples of the kinds of friendship loss I described earlier, they were so good for my soul and my development in the time I had them—and I for them as well. I truly cherish the memories of our times together.

God provided other friends along the way, too, so that I had good male companionship throughout my single years and up until the time I began dating my husband. I think of Tony (#1) and Chris from my church in Madison, good guys I still love today. Tony and I would rollerblade together. We'd tell each other of our dating escapades, and for some years, we'd pray together for that special spouse to come along for the other person.

Chris and I and others formed a cooking club. I can never forget the introduction he gave me to tiramisu. And Chris taught me how to mountain bike in the woods near my house (okay, I only did it one time!). These guys are still precious to me, and I can always call them and pick up where we last left off. One is married with a gaggle of kids, and the other is single at the time I'm writing this.

On the west side of Madison, there were David and Adam and Aaron and a group of adventurers I served with and laughed with. David shared an interest in missions. Adam and Aaron were brothers, the kind that are so opposite you wonder how they could come from the same womb. One had a serious personality and the other couldn't seem to take *anything* seriously! I'm still Facebook friends with all of them today.

There were Tony (#2) and Brian (#2) and Steve, all whom I met via a Christian camp called Fort Wilderness. There was even a Tony (#3) who was not as close of a friend, but we all had fun numbering our Tonys when a group of us were together. Tony (#2) was a dear friend who often found something to tease me about. We had a lot of good laughs together. He also was kind and once put gas piping into my home for me for free when I received a free gas stove from another friend. Steve had a special way of calling out people's strengths and is a good friend today.

Brian #2 was a friend who loved to bake and to cross-country ski. We once made a fun cookie table* video together for a newly married Pennsylvania couple when Tony (#2) dragged a group of us with him to a relative's wedding. I invited Brian to come with me to a Jerry Seinfeld performance in downtown Madison, only to discover that he was the only person in the auditorium that didn't think Jerry was funny. "Now that's funny."

Man, I still love these guys and cherish the memories of good times.

There was Scott whom I met on a big camping trip; I loved to have him over to cook together. As a pathologist, he had a habit of calling his friends by malady-inspired monikers that he derived from our names: Marilyn was "Mariloma." Ken was "Kencer." I had the privilege of his calling me "Anneroids." Yuck!

---

* More about cookie tables: "The Tradition of the Cookie Table," *Youngstown Live* (blog), April 25, 2019, https://youngstownlive.com/the-tradition-of-the-cookie-table/.

Scott and I had a similar sense of humor and did some fun trips together over time.

Two more good friends Paul and Brian #3 did wonderful work on my first house for very reasonable prices. One of them refinished the wood floors throughout the downstairs, and the other did renovations to my front porch. Brian had a knack for teasing me, and Paul was a big sweetheart.

I think of Jeff from when I lived in Maryland and the Spanish and French lessons we gave each other. What an enjoyable friend he was, especially for his willingness and vulnerability to be astonished at things he didn't know but might have known. I suppose he could admit to those things because he was a genius. For Jeff, I would sing a little ditty to the tune of the *Spider Man* theme song: "Digit Man, Digit Man, if Jeff can't calculate it, no one can."

There were other Maryland guys too. A group of them along with a bunch of gals helped me start a single adult ministry at our church. I think of Mark and Clint and Chad and a whole lot of other guys and gals that hung out at the home of my dear friend Kimberly. Chad came with me to a Josh Groban concert in Washington, DC, one year. He liked to say afterward that I took him on a date with 50,000 women. Even Josh Groban joked that "the ten men at the concert were all huddled together in the back of the arena."

I can't help but mention some special friends from my earlier teens and twenties too. Chuck and I were good friends who lived in the same dorm "house" for a couple of years in Ogg Hall at the University of Wisconsin–Madison. We became involved with the same campus ministry our first year.

One semester, early on Saturday mornings, we used to get up and go to the Memorial Union for a missions meeting. We'd sing lyrics from *Oklahoma*'s "Oh, What a Beautiful Morning," and he'd scoop me up in his arms and spin down the sidewalk. And then there was the time he was my secret Santa in a dorm house Christmas gift exchange, and he convinced me that I had one of the football players instead. So many nostalgic memories with Chuck. He was truly like a brother to me.

Jim was another friend that I loved dearly. Like a big brother, he was older, comfortable, and just so fun to tease. He and I would sit at the dorm piano and sing harmonies.

A guy named Rich and I spent time together in my last years of college and for a few years after that. He was a neighbor I had invited to a Friday evening church event who came to the Lord that night, even though he had been poking quite a bit of fun at the event's title beforehand (it had the word miracle somewhere in its title).

We had so much fun together over the years, whether talking about faith, praying, playing games, or pulling pranks on people. Rich was like a little brother to me. Eventually, he married and moved away, but there were other friends to come!

> I'm so thankful for the many, many guy friends God sent my way.

Steve was a good friend from my mid to late twenties. He was a handsome guy who was an open book with others. He lived in my neighborhood, and we took walks through the nearby zoo together. He was good at challenging me when I needed it. Jack was another friend from the same time period. He was a big guy with a big heart for the Lord and for people. Like me, he still had some middle school humor left in him! Jack joined me in on some of the pro-life work I was doing in those days.

There you have it. God sent these and many other friendships my way, both before and after his promise to do so, to bring that male influence into my life in my single years. And he sent me just as many wonderful gal friends. All these people I hold near and dear to my heart.

Looking Back

I'm so thankful for the many, many guy friends God sent my way over the years to fulfill his promise to me and to fill the void of male companionship. Some of these guys were interested in me at times and vice versa. One of them even told me he hoped to find someone like me but closer to his age. One told a mutual friend that I made his shortlist of marriage material. And me? I liked five of them in varying degrees. But I'm not telling who!

Ten

GILMAN HOUSE

Age twenty-nine. I lived with my husband for a year in 1990. That year, twenty-one years before he and I would begin dating, a group of single adults from our church's college and career group decided to rent a big house with four apartments. It had been a Tudor Revival* style home built around 1910, across the street and down the hill from what was the Governor's mansion until 1950. But now, it was pulling in forty thousand a year as a four-apartment, off-campus rental.

We dubbed it The Gilman House for the simple reason that it was located on Gilman Street. We set aside two apartments for men and two for women. I joined in the fun and lived in one of the first-floor apartments with three unique women: Tina, Carol, and Hitomi.

Tina and I were roommates and had a good friendship. She had one of those personalities that genuinely cared about other people with a superhuman love and other-centeredness. She eventually married one of the guys in the house, just as I did, but she did it in "real time" rather than two decades later!

---

* My architecture-loving husband made me add these details. *Made me!*

Then there was Carol, the girl who blew us all away with her knowledge of football statistics. She was a faithful fan of the sport and the only woman I've ever met who loved football so passionately. She could also sing any sitcom theme song or TV commercial jingle we could throw at her. She was vivacious and fun and also fell in love with and married—also in real time— one of the guys who moved into the house the next year.

> She eventually married one of the guys in the house, just as I did, but she did it in "real time" rather than two decades later!

Hitomi was a South Korean who had grown up in Japan. She was such a fun roommate and, over time, became a lifelong friend. I can never forget the packages of Japanese "junk food" her mom would send, including little packages of Ritz crackers individually wrapped in cellophane to protect the dried cheese spread and the single anchovy fish that was placed in the middle of the cheese. We couldn't believe she could eat those fish, and she would purposefully stick them out of her mouth and rub them along her lips to gross us out. It worked.

Across the hall was a guys' apartment where David, Jonathon, Rick, and John lived. David had one of those open-door kinds of hearts. He'd start sharing a story about something tender and get all teary-eyed. Despite his balding head, which he made a lot of jokes about, he was a catching fellow with his big brown eyes and long lashes. He eventually married Tina!

Jonathon was younger and full of life and excitement but also was a sensitive, sharing guy. Like me, he came from a large family, and we all knew several of his siblings. He could play guitar and piano really well and had a knack for listening intently to people.

Rick is someone that I honestly didn't get to know very well. I don't remember much about him from those years. John was a super-smart person, and we're still Facebook friends today. He is analytical and uses that skill today to make pointed arguments on his Facebook posts.

On the second floor was another guys' apartment. There were four men for four bedrooms, but they rented out a small closet with enough room for only a bed to a fifth roommate who was willing to take it so he could live with them. I hope they charged him an exceptionally low rent! The guys who lived here were Sean, Mark, Paul, Paul, and Steve (in the closet).

Sean was a smart fella finishing a PhD in microbiology. Cute as the dickens and possibly the one that had pulled us all together, he was likely the oldest among us as a thirty-something-year-old. He was an enthusiastic leader in our college and career group and loved to make people laugh with funny stories and imitations of French accents.

Mark and Paul were brothers: Mark was about four years younger than I, and Paul was even younger. Mark was a musician and wrote the music to at least one song specifically for a church event. He was always grinning and laughing with puppy-like enthusiasm (and I mean this in the best of ways). Paul was incredibly intelligent, yet also super sweet and just so funny. He wasn't around as much as others because he was the technical director for a big Christmas production at church, where he spent a lot of his time. Mark and Paul had funny voice-over videos of Star Trek episodes that kept us all laughing.

The second Paul was a sensitive guy who loved to laugh and to tease people. He was a good looker that many girls swooned over. But he was also serious about his faith and wrote the lyrics to one of Mark's songs. Paul also gave us free haircuts!

Steve was a handsome guy who was an open book. His proclivity for self- and life analysis was only surpassed by my own. He and I and another friend named Heather, who didn't live in the Gilman House, might have slowed down each other's ability to roll with the punches of life. So much navel-gazing! But I can picture Steve laughing and getting excited about something in his own unique way.

The second girls' apartment was on the fourth floor, where lived Jamie, Jerilyn, Liesa, and Shani. Jamie in a way was the house captain. I remember her as being engaged with the people in Gilman House much more than I was.

Jerilyn was the person who amazed me by saying that she would be happy if she could stay in school for the duration of her life. She loved to study and learn. She was one of those people with that wry sense of humor whose jokes hit you on the back end as you were walking out the door.

Liesa was a smarty and a cutie that went on to get a job as a meteorologist, and Shani was a sweet and shy young woman.

Over the year, we discovered that there were three pairs of people in the house with the same birthday. Amazing. And my future husband and I were one of those pairs.

Looking Back

It's fun to see the many ways my husband and I crossed paths in those years. One fun memento from the Gilman House related to us is that for Christmas, I purchased some plain mugs to paint with others in the house and give to each person. My husband was an art student, so we painted on his mug his name and an artist's paint palette. When he and I married twenty-three years later, that mug showed up with his things, and we still have it today!

Eleven

LEARNING TO BETTER LOVE MYSELF

Ages thirty-one and thirty-two. A good friend told me the truth I needed to hear. I had moved out of the Gilman House in 1991 because a friend, Julie, whose husband, Doug, traveled for work for weeks at a time, had asked me to live with them to keep Julie company. It worked out well because I was able to take a cool job with a French exchange program that paid well but not until months passed and ninety French high school students had come to the United States. They stayed for three summer weeks with the host families I had secured during the school year. Even better, I became closer friends with Julie.

The next year, I moved out of Julie and Doug's home and into a small one-bedroom apartment on Madison's east side. Julie came over one day to help me stencil a border in the kitchen—all the rage at that time. We were painting teal geometric shapes around the ceiling to match my teal tablecloth, teal dishcloths, and teal kitchenware. You get the teal picture.

I was telling her about a negative comment someone had said to me that had me down and questioning my worth. You know how it is—sometimes we humans are just in a bad mood and treat others rudely, maybe just because we're "hangry."

And yet, I would interpret these interactions as though they indicated how that person felt about me or what my value was.

Julie's response was pointed. "Annie, you need to learn to like yourself for who you are, no matter what others feel or say to you. As long as you're looking for others to tell you that you're worthwhile, your view of yourself will go up and down."

No one had ever stated such a concept so directly. It might be something that a lot of us learn when we are still a child, a teen, or a young adult. But for me, and for plenty of others, too, it comes later in life. As Julie spoke, I got it!

> "As long as you're looking for others to tell you that you're worthwhile, your view of yourself will go up and down."

The choice of loving ourselves and warding off the sting of negative interactions is simply to accept and believe the last phrase in Psalm 139:13-14: "For you created my inmost being; you knit me together in my mother's womb. I praise you because I am fearfully and wonderfully made; your works are wonderful, *I know that full well*" (emphasis added).

I had been familiar with these verses, but Julie was the first person that challenged me to appropriate it in terms of loving (and liking!) myself no matter what others said or did.

God loves us unconditionally, and we should do the same, take ownership of how we appropriate God's love for us. Stop relying on others to confirm God's value of us by their interactions, by their value of us, or by the mood they are in. It even means that when someone else says something that feels as though it devalues us, our own appreciation for who we are can rise up and fend off any suddenly incurred doubt of our worth.

Also, I didn't have to get the entire world to like me because I could like myself for my strengths and in spite of my weaknesses. Julie's words that day brought a welcome change. I immediately began putting this concept into practice.

About this same time, I heard a radio message from a biblical teacher named Chuck Swindoll. He encouraged his listeners to pray and to reach for spiritual maturity, emotional stability, and financial security. The message resonated with what Julie had said. The suggested prayers were good themes for growth toward maturity, so I began to pray them regularly.

Also in this season, a third factor was at work. I had begun working for a woman who came to be and still is a close friend. Liz is like an amateur counselor, and wherever she goes, people pour out their hearts to her. There's something about her response that's so accepting and loving to others that she is a balm of healing to

Pastor Swindoll has an article that cites Ephesians 4:14–15 and states that while we never arrive at being perfectly mature, it's the extremes of immaturity that dissipate as we mature. Seasoned confidence replaces "uneasy feelings of insecurity." We consistently move toward emotional and spiritual adulthood. We leave childish and adolescent habits and adopt a lifestyle where we are fully responsible for our own decisions, motives, actions, and consequences. In a word, maturity is stability.*

---

* Pastor Chuck Swindoll, "Marks of Maturity," *Insight for Today,* November 8, 2018, https://insight.org/ resources/daily-devotional/individual/ marks-of-maturity1/.

many. Women from all walks of life have been blessed to volunteer or work for her.

When Liz and I first began working together, she used to tell me what a special person I was, and I would literally say, "Oh Liz, you'll figure it out in time, like everybody else does, that I'm not such a great person." She would respond incredulously and say, "Annie, what are you talking about? You are a *wonderful* person; I'm not going to suddenly realize you're not!"

It wasn't as if people just up and left friendships with me. Thinking back to that time, I'd say the expectation that someone would stop liking me arose from a few experiences of people trying to influence a negative habit of mine and my stubborn resistance to change. I resisted even when more than one person made it clear that a tendency was irritating. I rejected these things because, as Julie helped me understand, I wasn't entirely accepting of myself warts and all. So those kinds of hints about irritating habits were not supportable yet.

As Liz kept telling me over months that I was a lovable, enjoyable person, I began to believe her and let go of my self-doubts. This combined with Julie's message to me and good old Chuck's admonitions, I was starting to claim the right to love myself. (And by the way, I can remember loving myself that way when I was very, very young, before the blows of life started to tear down the sense of being lovable.)

When I look back at this trifecta of the influence of Julie, Chuck, and Liz coming together, I see the hand of God working to heal my heart. And I began to work *with* him to shed my negative expectations. I was saying adieu!

One of the first results was that I could finally relax and admit that one of my tendencies was indeed irritating! I finally admitted to myself that friends were right when they told me I talked too loudly. I DID TALK TOO LOUDLY! I HAD BEEN

RAISED IN A FAMILY OF EIGHT KIDS. THE ONLY WAY TO BE HEARD WAS TO RAISE THE VOLUME!

For years, when people told me to quiet down, that they could hear me fine, I didn't love myself enough to just say, "Yeah, I'll quiet down. Sorry! I get carried away." Since I was relying on people to cue me in on my worth, if I heard them tell me to lower my voice, I had a defensive reaction. Since they don't like something about me, they must be telling me I'm worth less than others. I can't receive this message. I'LL TALK AS LOUDLY AS I WANT TO TALK! I'M NOT GOING TO TRY TO FIT IN!

Ah, humans. We're so complicated.

Looking Back

I'm a bit sad for that younger me who wasn't confident in who she was, for the times I didn't think I had a "seat at the table." And too bad I didn't recognize sooner that a little time with a therapist could help process my vulnerabilities to others' opinions and get on the path to healing. A therapist once helped me figure something out in a handful of sessions that decades of analysis with friends could never pinpoint.

Twelve

A GIFT FROM HEAVEN

Age thirty-four. Has God ever sent you a tangible birthday present? Remember the vision I described having when I was twenty-four years old about the snow and my beautiful, bright orange Pinto station wagon? Spring to the future with me when a wonderful, even miraculous gift was given to me that harkened back to that vision. It truly seemed God had given me a tangible birthday gift.

In 1995, as I turned thirty-four, I found myself as single as ever. There were significantly fewer eligible Christian men available, and my fertility clock ticked louder and louder. You might know what I mean. As I approached my birthday, God did something special. He dropped a personal gift into my lap, seemingly right from heaven, to encourage me that marriage was an option for me and was indeed in my future. It was another nudge toward a more positive expectation.

I explained earlier how in that vision from God, he had labeled a pair of white gloves that were given to me as "wedding gloves" and how one pastor counseled me that the vision would be understood when whatever the gloves represented became a reality.

The pastor's comments aside, many friends who heard the vision encouraged me to see that the gloves likely meant God was telling me I'd be married someday, despite my doubts. I wanted to believe it as strongly as they believed it! In fact, I kept this vision in the back of my mind all through the years I was single, and I hoped that all these friends were right about what the gloves meant.

And now it was ten years later, March of 1995, and my upcoming birthday reminded me I wasn't getting younger. I wondered about my future. I was living with a family I knew—the arrangement was a financial blessing for them and for me. For part of the time there, I slept in a basement room. I know this is every teen's dream—to have a room in the basement. But for me, the situation was not the future I had envisioned when I was younger.

My heart waxed cynical as I thought to myself, *Wow, I've really made something of myself. Not only am I so far from my dream of marriage and children, but I'm not even in my own apartment.*

This was my situation as I approached my thirty-fourth birthday. My heart wandered to the memory of the vision with the gloves and the hope in my heart to have a husband, a partner in life to share a home with. So, I talked to God about it one day.

"God, can we talk about singleness again? Well, about marriage? I'm feeling so far from reaching my life dreams. You know that vision you gave me with the orange Pinto wagon and the red shovel and the sparkly white gloves? A lot of people try to convince me that the gloves meant that I'll be married. And it seems that you yourself are telling me to keep praying because there is someone for me. So . . . I'm just asking . . . if the gloves and the dream meant that I'll someday have a partner to go through life with, and if you want me to confidently believe that, could you send an emblem from the vision my way? Not sure what I am expecting. A red shovel? A toy that looks like an old Pinto wagon? Could you just send something from that vision to say, 'Yes! The vision does mean you will be married some day!'"

I believe this was a question God dropped into my heart so he could answer it. In fact, from my point of view, he had set things in motion three months earlier to answer it.

Here's what I mean. Soon after, I got together with a friend I hadn't seen in a long time. She brought with her a Christmas present for me that she'd had in her possession for three months. I opened it to see a scarf and pair gloves designed for Christmas as she apologized that the gift was a bit moot since it was now March and not December. The scarf was black with gold threads sewn into it.

> But the gloves! They were white with gold glitter thread sown in so that they, too, sparkled.

But the gloves! They were white with gold glitter thread sown in so that they, too, sparkled. And although the gloves didn't end at the base of my hand, the white coloring did as it met a black border that went around the wrist. No pearl button, but definitely reminiscent of the sparkly white gloves of my vision. I was flabbergasted (gobsmacked, as the British say).

God had literally heard my request and sent me not just any token from the vision but a token that harkened to what he had called "wedding gloves" in the vision.

Can I say it again? I felt as if this gift had just dropped down from heaven! And I loved that the gloves had been purchased months earlier and then delivered when I asked for something extremely specific. This was a time my heart began to turn and expect that I would indeed find love in my future. I truly began to believe that God wanted me to know there was a future partner and family for me. But little did I know that it would still be another long wait. Yikes!

Looking Back

I'm so thankful for the memory of the gloves that came down right from heaven to my heart. In fact, as I type, those very gloves are four feet behind me, laid out on a piece of furniture along with a few other precious mementos. What a precious gift.

Also, while I was sleeping in that basement, I had no idea that one day I would marry a man who was already a friend at that time, one I had known for five years—a guy with a creative soul. I didn't know that right about the time I was moving out of that basement, a woman was refurbishing a newly bought, beautiful Queen Anne home in a town called Baraboo—repairing cracked walls; stripping and varnishing beautiful oak trim, floors, and doors throughout; adding a garage; and so much more. I didn't know that my husband-to-be and I would eventually each move to Baraboo, buy our own homes, and go on to sell them and buy the refurbished and renovated 1902 Victorian together, as our married starting point. God would make up for lost time.

Thirteen

THERAPIST FAILURE

Age thirty-five. What's wrong with me?! In my thirties, as a person that wanted to marry but hadn't found the right person, like others in a myriad of situations, I asked this question of myself. I don't vouch for that thought pattern, but sometimes it's there. In fact, some of us can spend quite a bit of time trying to get to the bottom of not reaching an elusive relationship goal by analyzing our shortcomings.

I do believe a person can reasonably ask, "Is there a reason I can't seem to find a life partner even though I want to find one? Even though I'm trying? Is there a barrier? Do I have a pattern or a blind spot?" Since it's human nature to have weaknesses, maybe we can ask ourselves these questions instead of, "What's wrong with me?"

I believe in finding the help of an appropriate therapist to get to the bottom of barriers to finding a relationship. They understand the psychology of relationships in ways the average person simply doesn't see as quickly. But for singles, it's important to query a therapist before meeting with them to learn if they have a heart to help singles find love and identify barriers to healthy relationships. Some therapists are caught up in the contentment superstition. I learned this the hard way.

In my mid-thirties, I found a Christian counselor with whom I hoped to discover and address my barrier(s) to finding true love. But unfortunately, this person was of the mindset that marriage as a goal for a Christian single was best addressed by ignoring it and pursuing other important life goals. In other words, her ambition for single Christians was to help them develop satisfaction or contentment with being single.

> It's important to query a therapist before meeting with them to learn if they have a heart to help singles.

Why not help a client pursue a lifelong love? It was funny, too, because all the aspects of life she wanted me to pursue were already in place, and the one area I wanted to pursue, she wanted me to ignore.

My short interaction with her set me back in my emerging desire to pursue finding a husband because her message supported what I had heard repeatedly: Be content with your single life. Focus on other areas of development. Let God do all the work in this one area, and you focus on developing all the other areas for your life—meaningful work, ministry, friendships.

I didn't meet with her a second time. It was as though I took a peek into the idea of trying to take steps toward finding love and had the door slammed in my face. But I didn't attempt to meet with another counselor either. First, I feared hearing the same message, and second, I wasn't making much money and had apparently gambled away some of it taking a chance on this therapist. How much would I have to spend just to be told again that working toward marriage as an actual goal was taboo in a counselor's mind? As bold as I could be, I wasn't bold enough for this.

Looking Back

I wish I'd had the confidence to query other therapists or to search for ones that would help me. But hey, the internet was a baby, and long-distance telephone therapy hadn't been invented yet, as far as I was aware. Using Google and online reviews wasn't an option. But even if it had been, I lacked the confidence to know that my goal to meet with a therapist to find and address my barrier to marriage was a good one. I couldn't yet escape the doubts that came from the contentment message.

Little did I know that far away in the state of South Carolina was a counselor I would meet in the future. She was growing in her experience of helping single adults overcome barriers to marriage and would one day help me!

Fourteen

PRAISING GOD THROUGH THE PAIN

Age thirty-six. He seemed like a perfect match for me. At thirty-six, I got to know a man who was involved with the same organization as I was. The man—I'll fictitiously call him Zach—was one of its prominent volunteers. I saw him regularly at events and was impressed with his service to the cause. He was good-looking and had a wry sense of humor. I was attracted to him and hoped he would have an interest in me too.

In time, however, he began to date someone that didn't share the same Christian faith he and I did, even though he had often vented that relationships between Christians and unbelievers didn't work. I thought, "Wow, he would rather date an unbeliever than me." But he met a gal, and he was smitten, so much so that all his platitudes went out the window. Who, me, bitter?!

I joke about it now, but at the time, I felt extremely rejected. I thought we could have served God together in this organization. It was the umpteenth time a potential love interest didn't go as I had hoped. And by that time, my biological clock was ticking so loudly that I look back and call it Big Ben. My heart felt broken—for all the times my interest in a man led to no results, for my diminishing dreams of raising a family, and most honestly, broken with a deep feeling of rejection.

Pains I had felt before, I could shake off with self-reminders of God's faithfulness, by turning to a good friend for prayer, and by hoping in the next opportunity.

> My heart felt broken—for all the times my interest in a man led to no results.

But this time, the pain was too deep. It threatened my future. How many more times could I meet interesting men only to be rejected?

My heart continued to ache for a couple of days, and I realized I had to do some serious spiritual battle. My feelings of despair were not acceptable! I decided that every day after lunch, I would close the door to my office and get down on my knees and worship God. And that's what I did. I played worship music and sang my heart out. And I cried. I poured out my feelings through the most honest words I could find. In between words, I sang. And in between songs, I cried. I prayed and wiped away tears.

This was undeniably a painful place. But I also knew that Jesus was my source of solace, my Rock,

By God's grace, I was always a fun and loving person and had *no business* lacking confidence in who God made me to be. But I hadn't yet *fully* learned the principle of taking ownership for loving myself, warts and all.

the one I could turn to in my quandary. And he delivered. Yes, he delivered me from my pain! One day, the third week into my worship-through-the-pain adventure, I climbed off my knees to find I was free from the pain. And in its place, joy. It was done. Jesus overcame the painful feeling of rejection! I had cried out to my Rock, and he pulled me out of the mud.

But something else occurred too. I received healing I didn't know I needed. As I got off my knees that day, I felt freedom from an inferiority complex I had carried. I stood up with new knowledge deep down inside that I was just as valuable as every other person. I also knew that I was just as valuable as every other woman who wanted to attract a good and godly man. I had no idea until this moment that I didn't already know this! But I certainly knew it now. It was as though the prayers and tears over those three weeks had seeped down past the momentary pain to the deep roots of rejection.

I am so glad I turned to God and not away from God in this crisis. His love and presence turned this experience into one of welcomed change and victory and a huge pillar in my history of faith. Yes, by the end of it, I was glad it had all happened.

Looking Back

There is a reason that research finds we are more secure the older we get. Those rare young people who are confident and at ease in their relationships even in their young adult years are truly blessed more than they probably understand.

Fifteen

JEALOUSY, MISERY

Age thirty-seven. I was jealous to the point of being miserable. With Zach long forgotten, I had met a guy who seemed to embody the qualities I desired in a husband. He loved the Lord and had a call to full-time ministry. I was convinced he was for me. I believe he spent at least a little bit of time entertaining the idea of asking me out.

At this time in my life, I thought that to receive from God a Christian leader husband, a gal should have to have a long history of consistently giving her life to Jesus.

So, when this guy was interested in and began dating someone who had only recently come to Christ after living a worldly lifestyle, I was jealous! I experienced the biblical proverb of "Anger is cruel and fury overwhelming, but who can stand before jealousy?" (Proverbs 27:4). I complained to God that this "wasn't fair." Why did someone who made those choices get a prize Christian guy like him? Why don't I get to date a guy like that since I've been making biblically-based choices for years, even decades?!

> "Anger is cruel and fury overwhelming, but who can stand before jealousy?" (Proverbs 27:4)

I was so upset that I sat down and wrote out my feelings to God, line by line. As I reflected on the thoughts behind them, I began to consider them quite silly. After all, none of us deserves anything in this life. I thought of the Bible's clarity that we can watch not only new believers receive more of God's blessing than we do, but we can even see ungodly folk find immense blessings from him. The Bible calls us not to worry when those who are opposed to God receive good things, the very blessings we think we deserve. Everyone's good gifts ultimately come from God. And without God, where would any of us be? Our part is simply to receive kind gifts despite our undeserving, self-serving ways.

As I compared my bitter words, written out, to the truthful messages I longed to hold more dearly in my heart, I began to laugh at myself. I needed an attitude adjustment. So, I finished off my rant with a plea for grace to get over my blues. Then I decided to turn my words into a song that I could sing the next time I encountered a similar temptation. Embarrassingly, all the lyrics except for the second chorus about receiving a great vocation (crafted to round out the song) were written from my heart. Yes, on that day and in those first hours, I truly felt all the hyperbole I wrote regarding how much more deserving I was than the other person in this situation. Well, praise God that by his Holy Spirit, I also wrote verse four—my repentance prayer—from the heart as well.

I called this song "Older Brother Blues" because Jesus told a story about a father and two sons in which the older brother was very jealous of the father's mercy given to the second brother when he returned home after a sinful path. The story was directed toward some self-righteous people in Jesus's community that didn't care for how kind and forgiving he was toward people they labeled as "sinners." The theme was similar to what I expressed in the lyrics of the song.

Older Brother Blues

I've been so faithful, Lord
I've walked with you so long
I've lain my life down every day
I've prayed, and I have fasted
I've given; I have lasted, Lord
Through all the trials that you send my way

But now this other Christian
Who lived a life of sinning
He went so far away from you
But now that he is come back
There ain't a thing that he lack, and
I've got the older brother blues

He's getting all your blessing
While I just sit here guessing
Exactly what I've got to do
To get your sole attention
About the things that I mention
That give me the older brother blues

Like, I just want a little money
Someone to call me honey
A house, a car, a TV or two
But you don't seem to hear me
I wonder if you're near me
Or too busy blessing your prodigal son

Like, I just want a great vocation
A deep-down inspiration
Respect at home, a little fame on the road
But you don't even see it
And I can hardly believe it
The way you bless him after all that he's done

Done, done, your prodigal son, yeah
That son of a gun

(*Musical interlude: a whining harmonica to
capture my childish tone*)

I don't mean to be so selfish
Just feeling on the shelf-ish
I need your grace to make me true
And you can be my honey
Don't need the toys or money
Just take away these older brother blues

And you can be my honey
Don't need the toys or money
Just take away these older brother blues
Take away these older brother blues
Take away these older brother, little boy blues

Looking Back

I recall the jealous feelings I had that day and wish I could
say I no longer experience those sentiments. When it came to
the interest of a man and the hope of marriage and children,
jealousy was definitely ready to raise its ugly head. For me, the

tenth commandment was then and will always be needed to bring me back to center: "You shall not covet your neighbor's house. You shall not covet your neighbor's wife . . . or anything that belongs to your neighbor" (Exodus 20:17). That about covers everything!

Sixteen

JACOB WEPT ALOUD

Age thirty-eight. I was living on the west side of Madison, attending a growing church and enjoying my first ever living wage job. There were some good men around. I was dating more than in my younger years when there had been even more men around. I had definitely made progress in my ability to attract a good man. But this came with a new challenge.

In my previous years, I had been insecure enough that anybody who spent time with me spoke confidently about their opinions and rarely expressed any self-doubt to me. They often responded to my own requests for assurances, whether verbal or nonverbal, with paternalistic words of advice. But as I grew into a more confident person and came into my own, people didn't seem as sure of themselves as they had in the past. I no longer offered the world a big confidence vacuum to fill. So, people were just normal—not parental but friendly with some insecurities.

And when it came to guys, I didn't know what to do with this normalcy. I didn't know how to date a person that showed any self-doubt. I wasn't used to it and was turned off. I can think of at least one relationship that ended partly because of this.

Eventually, I adjusted to the real world of relationships. In fact, leap ahead to the future, the day my husband and I first discussed dating each other. He let out with some big statement about a weakness he had, but by then, I wasn't thrown by such a statement. I gave him the reassurance he needed in the moment, and we went on our merry way.

> As I grew into a more confident person and came into my own, people didn't seem as sure of themselves.

But in my late thirties, such expressions were new to me. So, I was thinking a lot about character and what human beings ("youman beans" in my dad's dialect) are truly made of. Some sugar. Some spice. Some things insecure and some things nice. I knew several single Christian men, and each one offered his own mix of personality, character, strength, and weakness. I wondered which mix my future husband might have.

With this backdrop, a question for God dropped into my heart. "God, can you give me a picture from the Bible of the man I will marry?" It was a question *for* God but also, perhaps, a question *from* God. I say this because immediately after asking, I heard a clear response in my mind to look up Genesis 29:11. So, I looked up the verse and found: "Then Jacob kissed Rachel and began to weep aloud."

I thought of Jacob and Esau, the twin brothers from the book of Genesis that were as different as tomato paste and ice cream. Esau was a mighty hunter and Jacob a chef. Esau was hairy. Jacob was smooth. Esau was especially loved by his father and Jacob by his mother. I read this passage and surmised that God was saying the man I'd marry would be a man with inside skills more than outside skills, maybe not a hunter but a man who could cook up a good batch of venison. But it turned out, this wasn't how the man Jacob was a picture of my future spouse.

I wouldn't find out until my first date with my husband, when he said something out of the blue about this very Biblical character. In that moment I was dumbfounded that God had told me so long beforehand what my husband decided to share that day. But for now, I took encouragement that God indeed knew the character of the specific man I'd marry someday.

Looking Back

I think about the questions God dropped into my heart that day. He did the same thing in the vision I experienced, as told in chapter 5, when I asked, "What style of gloves are these?" What if other questions we carry or bury are actually questions that God has placed in our hearts so that we'll ask them and receive an answer? This reminds me of the admonition in James 1:5-6: "If any of you lacks wisdom, you should ask God, who gives generously to all without finding fault, and it will be given to you. But when you ask, you must believe and not doubt, because the one who doubts is like a wave of the sea, blown and tossed by the wind." God help us to bring our questions to him in confidence and not in fear and doubt!

Seventeen

YOU THINK YOU'RE TOO OLD, BUT GOD...

Age thirty-nine. "I'm too old to find anyone." That thought was beginning to find its way into my mind as I headed toward the finishing year of my thirties. A chapter of opportunity was coming to an end. My dream to meet the right one continued to elude me. I was tempted to give up. It felt as though I were the only one in the family, in my group of friends, in my Bible study, in my whole town who was still waiting for what others took for granted. All around me, friends and family experienced life in a normal timeline. Some days, I felt left out in the cold.

Turning thirty-nine coincided with aging out of what I considered the last child-bearing years of my life. Even though I wanted to adopt children, I also monitored Big Ben attentively because I would have loved and cherished the privilege, and miracle, of bearing a child. But it was at the very least becoming a risky proposition.

To encourage myself that good things were still to come and that what God had said would happen *would indeed happen*, I thought about the father of the nation of Israel, Abraham himself, not to mention his wife Sarah, who acutely experienced this feeling of grasping at water when it came to their goal of building a family. I put myself in their sandals. What would it be like to be a couple in their eighties and nineties, "dried up" (we know what that means), and trying to believe a promise from God that they were yet to bear a child?

> All around me, friends and family experienced life in a normal timeline. Some days, I felt left out in the cold.

The pain Abraham and Sarah faced in not bearing their promised heir, year after year and decade after decade, was so bad that they implemented a plan that we nonchalantly read about but would shudder at if it happened in our time. Sarah "gave" Abraham her slave/servant Hagar as a second wife to sleep with so that Sarah could "have a child" through Hagar. It was a classic case of desperate times leading to desperate measures. Understandably, this didn't solve their problem; it only led to more pain.

But behind all their shenanigans, God was still on the throne. Eventually, several years after Hagar's son was born, God's promise was fulfilled. Sarah bore the promised son. God had had a plan during all their years of waiting and frustration and misguided effort. And he made his promises to them come to be.

For me God had dropped the vision of snow and the physical gift of the wedding gloves. And a year earlier he had given me a picture of the man I'd marry in a Bible verse about Jacob kissing Rachel. Was I going to believe or to doubt? I wanted to trust God's repeated promises in spite of the fact that getting so close to the age of forty was tempting me to doubt. My circumstances told me I was too old to find a good Christian man in my age range. But God's Word and the testimony of Abraham and Sara showed me otherwise.

At this time, thankfully, God gave me another promise that I would find Mr. Right. Yes, to my comfort, God brought me another situation that showed me how much he cared about my life and dreams for my future. It wasn't only that I would eventually marry but also that there would be a certain quality in the love my husband would bring.

The promise came to me through an amazing spiritual gift described in Paul's first letter to the Corinthians as a word of knowledge, one of the supernatural gifts that God gives to the body of Christ:

> Now about the gifts of the Spirit, brothers and sisters, I do not want you to be uninformed. . . . There are different kinds of gifts, but the same Spirit distributes them. There are different kinds of service, but the same Lord. There are different kinds of working, but in all of them and in everyone it is the same God at work. Now to each one the manifestation of the Spirit is given for the common good. To one there is given through the Spirit a message of wisdom, to another a message of knowledge by means of the same Spirit . . . These [gifts] are the work of one and the same Spirit, and he distributes them to each one, just as he determines. (1 Corinthians 12: 1, 4–8, 11)

Though I've shared about other times when God communicated his word to me through others, the nature of this experience was a bit different, a bit stronger and bolder. In fact, I had gone to an event at a local church in Madison to attend a session the church offered about the gift of knowledge and how to maturely manage any bits of supernatural knowledge that God might throw our way for ourselves or for others. I'm sure that the staff of the hosting church could imagine how wrongly a word of knowledge might be shared with another person and, even more, had witnessed it. And so, they offered this unique workshop, one I didn't see or hear of very often.

The biggest key I recall from the session was to manage words of knowledge that I believe are from God for another person with extreme humbleness and awareness of my frailty as a human. For example, I could say, "I believe God has given me a word for you, that he is saying such and such about your life. Does this make sense to you? Does your heart agree that it applies to your life? Or did I just have too much pizza sauce last night?" It's ultimately up to the person to discern whether God is speaking in what I share, not up to me.

After the presentation, we formed groups to pray for one another and to practice listening for and speaking out anything God might say to us for each other. I suppose because we were in this workshop together, and because each of us welcomed the prayers and, hopefully, the divine insight from God through each other, there wasn't as much practice with asking each other to confirm what we thought God was saying. In fact, given to me was a word that the person gave so loudly and authoritatively, it almost embarrassed me. But I recognized it and knew it to be God's voice from the way the situation played out.

In my group of five, as in the other groups, each of us took a turn in the hot seat to be prayed for. In the role of praying for another, it was a special time of *listening* to God in prayer, carefully, with spiritual ears turned on, instead of *talking* to God in prayer without giving him a chance to talk back. I can recall praying for the others in my group, sometimes "hearing" a word for some and sometimes not. But for each person, there were some words that God gave.

I was the last one in the hot seat, and before my turn, I whispered in my heart to God what I would love to hear him address. I did not speak a word about these things to the others. In fact, I didn't know any of them except for one guy named Al, who had been in the same college and career group as me a decade earlier. But I confided to Jesus a private prayer, saying, *I would love it if you spoke to me about marriage and about my work.*

When it was my turn to be prayed for, that's exactly what happened, and that's why I believe it was indeed God speaking, once again, addressing the questions in my heart. One person received a word for me about marriage and work. And two others also received a word about work. It was my old acquaintance Al who spoke first, and it was all about marriage. And by the way, Al is the one who practically shouted out his words for everyone to hear. People could have heard it two groups away from us! True, the workshop didn't address this aspect of how to deliver. Ah, but such is life; nothing is perfect.

Standing behind me with his hand on my shoulder, Al spoke these words: "Annie, God loves you so much. Annie, God is going to bring you a husband who is going to love you and cling to you, Annie. Yes, he's going to love you and cling to you! You think you're too old and past the normal marrying age, but God has a unique plan for you, Annie. God has a unique plan for you and one that is in a different timeline than other people's timelines."

Wow! I was amazed that God not only continued his encouragement to me that marriage was in my future but he also addressed how I was feeling old as far as my chances of finding true love. God met me where I was.

Al went on to share a word about my job. And after this, two women in the group also received words of knowledge for me about my job. These were also precious to me.

Not one shared a word about any other subject—just the two I had asked God for. As I sat for the final closing remarks, I was thankful that God had answered my specific prayers. My conviction that I would eventually find love deepened by several notches that night.

> Pouring out my heart to God about my cares often led to comfort and relief.

Experiences like this make me encourage others to take all their thoughts, feelings, pains, and temptations to Jesus and let him speak about them. If only we wouldn't hide them from God or tell ourselves that God is sick of hearing about them. When I believed he was sick of my broken-record prayers and subsequently refused to bother him with my lonely thoughts, these were the occasions that led to bitter feelings.

On the other hand, pouring out my heart to God about my cares often led to comfort and relief. And sometimes, it led to promises from God regarding my future.

By the way, I'm not sharing how God's gift of the word of knowledge worked in my life as a way to idolize the gift. It's just one more part of my story of how God spoke to me about my heart's desire, and it meant something to me. It still does. And I know he can speak to anyone at any time if he chooses.

Also, I'm sure it isn't wrong to ask him to speak to us, but it doesn't mean he will do so in the way we desire or that he'll necessarily say what we want to hear. And on the other side of the coin, sometimes he chooses to speak to us, but we either don't recognize his voice or refuse to listen. If only we'd improve our ability to line up his speaking and our hearing and listening to happen at the same time!

Looking Back

The words of knowledge I received that day had interesting timing. God alone would have known as they were spoken that something was going to happen within weeks with my husband-to-be that would eventually become one of the ties that would bind him to my heart.

In March, as I finally turned the dreaded thirty-nine, it coincided with my looking for a house to purchase in a town I previously mentioned called Baraboo. Located about an hour north of Madison, where I was living, Baraboo offered quaintness and cuteness and close proximity to the country.

One day, I nonchalantly asked a longtime carpenter friend of mine to meet me in Baraboo to look at a certain house and provide an assessment of its condition. This is one of the guys who, ten years earlier, had been a housemate!

Little did I know that day as we looked the house over, he was the one that would someday love me and cling to me as had been spoken just a few short weeks previously through Al.

My future husband walked confidently through the house as a man would do. And I noticed! He knew what to look for and how to assess what he saw in the house. And he just *saw* things. For example, looking at the heating and cooling vents and then at the furnace down in the basement, he pointed something out.

Husband-to-be (HTB): Wow, I've never seen anything like this.

Me: What?

HTB: This house's cold air returns and heating ducts are reversed!

Me: Huh?

HTB: The house was built in . . . 1940 did you say?

Me: Yeah?

HTB: Well, back then, the cold air returns were always built into the outside wall. But this house has it reversed.

Me: And?

HTB: Oh nothing. Just weird. I don't know why they did it. Might not be as efficient.

Me: Something to worry about?

HTB: No, nothing to reject the house over. Just *weird*.

I was impressed with his knowledge. But was I smitten with love for my old friend? No, nothing changed in my or his heart that day. But I can't help but reflect now, as I look back, how each room had a story to come.

We went into the kitchen, where he examined the windows for air leaks and searched for cracks in the walls. But we didn't see the days to come with the two of us, growing in friendship, sitting at the table working on a grant application or standing by the stove, experimenting with how to make the best bananas foster we could muster.

> We had no idea that in that very room, still far off in the future, we'd be sitting on a big, L-shaped brown leather couch, discussing whether we should date.

In the living room, we stood looking at the fireplace, wondering whether the flue was open and safe. We had *no idea* that in that very room, still far off in the future, we'd be sitting on a big, L-shaped brown leather couch, discussing whether we should date.

And over in the bathroom, we looked at the old worn sink base and decided it worked but wasn't very reflective of the period in which the house was built. We didn't know that one day, we would be engaged, and he, as my fiancé, would be replacing that sink and renovating the whole bathroom to help sell the house and help us buy our dream home together.

Yes, God had, unbeknown to me, given me just a few weeks earlier a word of knowledge about *this* guy. *This man* would love me and cling to me. Ah, but I couldn't see it at the time. There was still a barrier between us that prevented any thoughts along the line of romantic expectations. But I sure did like him as a friend.

Eighteen

PATIENCE, DONKEY, PATIENCE

Age thirty-nine. Did you ever hear the prank that sassy joke tellers like my mother used to share about the farmer and the donkey? My mom told it at a big family party to a group of us kids once, and she got me! It went down like this:

> Mom: And now I'd like to tell you all a story in four parts. Act 1. Long ago, in a world that is no more, a farmer and his donkey were traveling to a town far away, over hills and through valleys. The donkey grew tired and cried, "Master, when will we get there?" But the farmer only replied, "Patience, jackass, patience." Act 2. When the donkey and the farmer had traveled ten more miles, the donkey cried, "Master, I'm tired! When will I get to lie down on some straw?" To which the farmer replied, "Patience, jackass, patience." Act 4. The next day when the donkey was getting hungry . . .
>
> Me: (gullible, thinking I'd caught a mistake) Wait! What happened to Act 3?
>
> Mom: Patience, jackass, patience.

Yes, it was a funny joke, but I couldn't believe my mother had just called me a jackass!

In my single years, while there were times that God spoke promises to me of the love that was to come, there were also times when he addressed a need to enjoy my life as it was while I waited. It was as though God were saying to me, "Patience, donkey, patience."

> There were also times when he addressed a need to enjoy my life as it was while I waited.

One particular day, as I was complaining to God that I was living life alone, he put on my heart to read Psalm 4. Verse three jumped out at me: "Know that the LORD has set apart his faithful servant for himself." I sensed him telling me to praise him that he had set me apart for himself for now. It wasn't something I wanted to do. But I couldn't deny the sense he was calling me to praise him for it. So, I did.

Later that morning, I happened to get in a conversation with an old friend who was raising children and homeschooling. She had a gaggle of children, and I was a little envious. I shared with her my efforts to praise God that he had kept me for himself for now. And she shared with me all the pressure she felt to meet each day's challenges in homeschooling her children while trying to manage the house and meals at the same time.

She longed for some carefree mornings while I hoped for the full life of a family with children. That day, we both had a glimpse of another person's struggles and a reminder that life can be hard whether we are single, married, or with or without children. We could all work to become more thankful for what we have, whether the freedom of singleness or the belonging of marriage. For all seasons, there is a time for patience.

Another time in this same period, my neighbor gave me a Kay Arthur study called *Lord, Heal My Hurts* to use in my devotions. I came to a chapter on forgiveness in which Arthur asked the reader to pray for help to remember anyone they were not forgiving for one thing or another. I prayed the prayer, and God answered. I dealt with it. Done deal. But next, Arthur asked us to think about things we are angry with God about. Then she gave a tough assignment. Just. Be. Quiet. And. Listen.

She predicted the reader would claim to have no anger with God, and I was truly right there. I thought, *Oh no, I'm not mad at God about anything.* I can still remember sitting quietly, waiting for what I thought would be nothing. And then, after five minutes, as clear as ever, I heard the Holy Spirit say, "You're impatient with God for a husband."

I heard my own voice shoot back, "Of course I'm impatient!! I'm almost forty!"

Wow.

It happened so fast. I was surprised to hear God pinpoint something in my heart and to hear my immediate response. It seemed the Lord was taking the opportunity to coax me toward more patience with his timing, more trust in his love, and less reliance on my own assessment of the right time to marry.

Looking Back

I think about how, at the age of two, my parents taught me that I was not allowed to have a temper tantrum and stomp my feet when I didn't get my way. "Go to your room if you insist on stomping your feet and come back when you're ready to be calm." The message was clear, and I remember the shock of it. What?! Not only did I not get what I wanted, but I wasn't allowed to express my disappointment by stomping and complaining and being rude about it?!

In a similar way, God called me out through the Kay Arthur study for being impatient with him for the timing of marriage. What?! Not only did I have to wait (and wait) for the right time to marry, but I also had to be patient? Alas, that is what he was calling me to. It was as though he were saying, "Since I'm supplying you with promises of a lifelong love, how about if you give me some respect and patience in return?"

And so, while there were many promises along the way for me to find love, there was also the challenge to be patient in the process. As I've made clear, I'm not talking about a pseudo promise of "once I was content, God would bring the man." God was just saying, "Patience, child, patience."

Nineteen

THE FIVE SOBS

Ages forty to forty-two. I came home to an empty house one evening and asked myself how it happened. *How is it that I'm living my life alone? Where are the children that should be climbing out of the family van and racing to the house to use the bathroom first? When is my dream for a family going to be realized?*

It isn't only single women who come home with this pain burning in their hearts. There is a silent pain born by many women, married or single, who held a lifelong dream of raising children but didn't wind up with that privilege (and I'm sure by many men as well). They might have tried to find that man to raise children with. They might have found him and tried to become pregnant to no avail. Maybe they couldn't afford infertility treatment or tried and failed.

For some, adoption efforts led to broken hearts, and they dared not try again. I know of people that married someone who supported and wanted to raise a child before getting married, but after the glorious day at the altar, later refused to have a child. In any case, somehow, through life's turns and twists, for these women, it didn't happen. A child did not come their way.

I'm one of the women who wanted to raise children but didn't achieve the goal. And I was all in. I thought about how I would raise my kids a lot. I practiced conversations in my head. *Focus on the Family*, a radio program for parents, was something I listened to weekly if not daily, over many years in preparation for raising kids.

For most of my life, I wanted to find someone with whom I could adopt children. Even at the age of fourteen, when I was standing next to my bedroom closet one day, I found myself asking God to match me with a man that couldn't have children because I would be happy to adopt instead. And yet, there was still that desire to bear my own children too.

In my early forties, Big Ben had grown obnoxious, ticking ever so loudly in my heart, insisting on dominating and making his presence known in so many of my conversations. Going to work each day at the state health department (I was now managing a statewide program to help teens delay sex, similar to the work I had done locally in the past), my closest colleagues were each getting pregnant in turn.

After having spent my twenties watching family and friends my age marry and start families, now I was watching colleagues who were ten years younger do the same. It was painful. I not only wanted to raise children, but I wanted to be a part of society, of the normal flow of life. A gal without kids can feel left out of the milestones of life and the hallmarks of what it means to be a woman. Not all women have these longings, but I surely did.

And now here I was. It was one of those evenings where a person deconstructs their life and compares it to their goals. And so, I came home after a day filled with pregnancy talk, maybe even a baby shower, with despair washing over me. The house was empty; there were no kids, no man.

While I was analyzing my life and asking how I ended up in this situation, my neighbor Liz happened to come by, and just as with Carla so many years before, a caring friend saw my distraught face and gave me compassion.

As I spilled my heart, the tears flowed, and Liz wrapped her arms around me. Then I lay my head on her shoulder and cried so hard that those tears can only be described as sobs. She let me soak her shoulder with salty tears and just listened. Eventually, the tears and my sobs simmered down. But the grieving process wasn't over.

> Then I lay my head on her shoulder and cried so hard that those tears can only be described as sobs.

Over a span of two years, as Big Ben roared on, as my periods grew wonkier and wonkier, and as my body gave increasing indications that its availability to conceive life was coming to an end, I understood the pain of a biblical woman named Hannah. She struggled with infertility and described her pain and her prayers to God in these words: "I am a woman troubled in spirit . . . I have been pouring out my soul before the LORD" (1 Samuel 1:15 ESV).

By the end of it, there were five friends that experienced my full-on sobbing as I, too, poured out my soul before the Lord. As I bathed their shoulders in salty tears, they didn't offer shallow "at least" statements that are so tempting to say: "At least you have other children in your life," or "At least you live in the twenty-first century when children aren't the definition of your femininity."

In due time, the "at least" types of comforting thoughts would come from me as self-care. Just to make myself laugh, I might have once told myself, "At least you don't have a hole in your head."

Fortunately, my comforters knew offering "at least" phrases wasn't their part. Instead, they listened, wrapped an arm around my shoulder, and let me sob and grieve. They didn't try to minimize the loss. And they prayed with me, too, letting God lead their prayers. I'm thankful for these friends when the pain of losing my ability to bear children was so acute.

Looking Back

Not having children still hurts sometimes. And I hurt for others I love and know who are childless. I care deeply for their loss of the dream. For some, I feel that pain daily.

Twenty

An Awakening

Ages forty-two to forty-four. They were too bright, too loose, or too tight, but they were IN! Do you ever look at old pictures of yourself and laugh at the clothes you were wearing? When gauchos became popular in my high school years, I thought they were the ugliest looking pants I'd ever seen, but six months later, I was styling them with pride!

The funny thing is, I was only wearing them because my sister-in-law had given me a bountiful box of stylish clothes she'd obtained as extras through a connection to the fashion industry. The larger story of my childhood fashion life was one of wearing third-hand clothes that had gone from my cousin Joann to her sister Rose, and a few years later, to me. Wearing the gauchos and other fashionable clothes that came from my sister-in-law was merely a pattern of wearing what I received.

As I began to earn my own money and could buy my own clothes, the outfits I put together, just like the clothes I had received, were hit or miss. Having been raised on free clothing, I was a sucker for a good deal and often talked myself into ill-fitting clothing because something was cheap, or I wanted something so badly that I tried to make the wrong size fit. In fact, not only in high school but for years afterward, I shopped with one thing in mind: find something inexpensive. I had learned as a child to make do with what was free; as an adult I practiced making do with what was cheap.

It was easy for me to ignore the value of style. There is plenty of talk in society and in the church about a focus on the outside appearance being surfacy and shallow, and I agreed. I focused on the many messages I would hear about the importance of inner qualities in attracting a mate (did I just say, "a mate"?).

> I came to understand that these efforts attention to dress and hairstyle are simply a part of self-care, not self-ambition.

I didn't understand the value of my physical appearance as a key to attracting a good man. In fact, I thought that making my *home* beautiful was more important than making *me* beautiful. Yes, I literally thought that men were looking for a wife that could make a lovely home. To be sure, this can be included on a man's wish list, but I thought it was as or more important to them than finding a physically attractive woman. I put it much further at the top than it deserved. Where did I get this idea? Not sure. Any short-term study into what a man wants in a woman will reveal that up near the top of his list are beauty and sex appeal—and beauty and sex appeal!

Over time, I came to understand that attention to dress and hairstyle are simply a part of self-care, not self-ambition. They're a signal to men (and to the world) that I care about myself and my appearance. By neglecting style and beauty, I was hurting my desire to marry. My attitude kept me from giving men a chance to care about the inside because my outside said I didn't respect the laws of attraction.

I woke up. I realized that I was a fool to think a man was looking for a beautiful home instead of a beautiful woman.* No longer could I tell myself, "Well, if a guy doesn't love me just as I am, then he's not the guy for me" or something similar. (When I used to say this, were others thinking, "Well, maybe you could make a *little* more effort"? But they didn't dare say it. It isn't the kind of thing we can say to each other unless there is a mountain of trust between us.)

So, I continued to value good character and making a beautiful home, but I also began to make more effort in having a good outfit to wear and a daily hairstyle. And it felt good!

Looking Back

I know there are some couples who seem drawn together *because* they don't focus on the surface things. More power to them! But for me, I realized whatever I was looking for and attracted to was what I should try to offer. And I was definitely more attracted to men that put some effort into their looks.

---

* My husband does appreciate my love for making our home beautiful, something we do together, but it is not the cornerstone of what drew us together!

Twenty-One

KIMBERLY'S PLACE

Ages forty-five to forty-six. The parties didn't start until ten in the evening. That's how life was with the friends that gathered at Kimberly's place. After moving to Maryland to take a job with the U.S. government (managing federal instead of state level grants) and trying for a year to establish a group of friends, I finally met my good friend Kimberly. She was about five years younger than I and had also been single and Christian for just about her whole life. Like me, she gravitated toward serving roles once she became established in a church. After all, there was plenty of connecting, leading, and relationship-building to be done in the kingdom of God.

At our church in Maryland, Kimberly was the part-time leader of the girls' half of a thriving youth ministry. She coordinated small group leaders and did oh, so much for the young people at our church. And everyone loved her—youth, parents, children, and a whole bunch of single adults that found a place to belong at her place. I was one of them.

The core people in this group of singles were in their thirties, and some of us were in our twenties or forties. But we all had a good time together. We did Bible studies, organized rafting trips, enjoyed concerts, and volunteered together. One year, many of us went to the Western Maryland forest for an Easter retreat that included a search in the woods for a hundred eggs. But the good times at Kimberly's were the best of times.

We'd gather at Kimberly's past the hour when most people were snoring in bed and stay until one or two in the morning. She owned a newer townhouse that she decorated in fun—purple and pink walls, dishware with stiletto shoe designs, flip-flops and zebra-striped knickknacks dotting the walls and shelves. We fell into super comfy, overstuffed furniture for a chat or pulled up to a table with cards and games. Kimberly's face was usually lit up with a big smile, and she always had a laugh ready to spill into the room.

> Kimberly's face was usually lit up with a big smile, and she always had a laugh ready to spill into the room.

Of course, there was always food to eat. We sometimes played games, but a lot of the time we just talked and laughed and teased each other and ate more treats. We were silly and giddy. Most importantly, we belonged. And we knew it.

I wrote the following song for Kimberly to honor the way she used her life, her time, and her home to make so many people find a place to belong while she waited for a lifelong family of her own. It was a place to find Jesus, a meal, a friend. And I tried to capture the unique things about her and her home that were endearing. "Kimberly's Place" reflects the spirit of believers everywhere who exercise the gift of hospitality and who give others, especially older single adults, a place to belong.

Kimberly's Place

Come with me to a place where faith is formed
Come with me to a home where lives are reborn
You'll meet a good friend who will love you as you are
And in her eyes, you'll see the bright morning star

Come see discipleship in a house with purple walls
Find hospitality anytime you call
Come have a meal served on ceramic stiletto shoes
Oh, pour your heart out, and she'll chase away your blues

Come to Kimberly's place, Kimberly's place
She's trying; she's dying to herself in every way
She's laughing; she's loving everyone she meets today
At Kimberly's place
Where Jesus's heart is worn

Come with me to a place where teens and children go
Come see them laugh with her, their faces all aglow
She's on the run with them to church or to the mall
She's pouring out her life; she's following the call

Come meet a soldier girl like many in her field
Her dreams are waiting, but her dedication's real
She looks to Jesus, for her life is in his hand
He gives her joy and strength to follow in his plan

Has anyone seen the passion of a soul sold out for Christ?
Has anyone seen the joy, the pain of laying down a life?

Where Jesus's heart is worn

(Original verse 4, very specific to our good times at Kimberly's place)

Come play a feisty game of cards to build your fame
Marshmallow shooting, "pitching tape"—just pick your
    game
She'll get the vacuum out to clean the floor—or play
She'll clean before we come and when we go away

Looking Back

Before and after my time in Maryland, there were other friendship groups during most of my single years. We supported each other spiritually and did ministry together. We had parties. We had fun. We fished in Canada, rafted down Wisconsin's Kickapoo River, and did plenty of camping.

Such groups are fluid and eventually die out after several years. But they are important for the years they thrive. And to flourish, a Kimberly is needed at the center of every friendship group—someone that opens up their doors to give others a home where they belong. Such people live out the call to "Contribute to the needs of the saints and seek to show hospitality" (Romans 12:13 ESV). I thank God for all the Kimberlys in the world!

Twenty-Two

MIDLIFE CRISIS

Age forty-six. Have you ever met someone you wanted to date but whose values just didn't align with your own? There's an attraction, a spark, an interest. But you know it just couldn't go anywhere because your values are so different, so you fight off the temptation.

Other times, even though a person is obviously not a match but is attractive in one way or another, we forge ahead. Against everything we have ever been taught about the importance of compatibility, we tell ourselves we can change the person or that God can change them through our affection. Or that we'll change ourselves for *them*. For anyone whose been there, done that—had that relationship that was destined to sour and leave them with regret—breaking someone else's heart can feel just as bad as being the one who's left behind.

Many of us, if not all, have watched friends we love make trepidatious dating choices. Some have even married a person who was not a good fit, and we knew it. Maybe those choices led to years of regret. Even lifelong sorrow.

I flirted a few times with trying to make a wrong man into a right partner along my thirty-three-year journey as a single adult. The time I spent with one guy in 2007 led to some good conversations with concerned friends about life choices and midlife crises.

I met him on a fluke. I heard him speaking French to someone as he was delivering food in a café where I was having lunch with a friend. I couldn't resist saying a few words to him in *la plus belle langue du monde.** He was from a Mediterranean country but living in Virginia while working on a master's degree in biology. He wasn't particularly handsome and a little too short and young for my taste, but he was friendly, and we enjoyed exchanging cultural insights about our countries.

I didn't develop the friendship because of an attraction to him but simply because of my love for cross-cultural relationships. We became friends and over the time of a year, spent more time together—usually with others but occasionally one on one.

After a while, this man talked of our dating despite our age difference, but I just laughed at him. I would only date Christian men, and he was too young for me. But his attentions flattered me, and that was the risky part.

> His attentions flattered me, and that was the risky part.

In fact, over time, I wondered about this guy's arguments to date him. It was a good feeling to hear them, and I began to ask myself and God if it were possible that he was the one God had promised me was coming. In a phone call, I shared thoughts about him with my long-time friends Dave and Peggy, who were back in Wisconsin. "Maybe the Lord wants to bring

* "the most beautiful language in the world"

us together so I can lead him to Christ and go back to his country with him and be a Christian light."

They were alarmed to hear me say this, and Dave didn't pull any punches, "To his country in North Africa!? You've got to be kidding."

They didn't buy the idea at all that God had brought along this friendship with the purpose of a relationship. Understandably, they didn't even throw me a bone that it wouldn't be a bad idea to share the gospel with him. Instead, they thought of other people they knew who were soundly established as Christians but threw away their Christian life or long-term marriages to chase after a far-fetched relationship.

Peg shared, "You know, Annie, I know women who have walked away from God and their families for an offbeat, blinding relationship, had a midlife crisis, and did a 180-degree turn away from God."

She knew it was plausible for a strong Christian woman to up and leave everything she held dear. And the way I was talking, she perceived I could also make a bizarre choice that came from a midlife crisis of lost dreams. She had learned that any woman she knew could end up authoring the next *How I Escaped Life in a Harem* memoir or some other retelling of a misguided relationship choice that led to a life upheaval.

Peg and Dave knew that the root of the temptation was likely a midlife crisis. They felt a good prayer shot in the arm— the inoculation of drawing close to Jesus to gain a new vision of God's love and call on my future—would help me resist the temptation to flirt around with a dead-end romance. In addition to praying on the phone with me, Dave asked, "When are you coming back to Madison? I'll bet Peg can get some gals together to pray with you about your life. The Lord could give you a renewed vision of the life ahead."

Peg joined in. "Oh, yeah, Annie, I can set up a special prayer session with some gals that are good at listening for God's heart and passing on his words of encouragement."

I wanted to protest that the temptation wasn't as serious as they were perceiving, but I also understood the mistakes others had made were real and heartbreaking. I knew that the power of prayer when joined with people who know how to hear from the Lord is life changing.

In early 2008 I flew from Maryland into Madison, Wisconsin for a weekend winter retreat with old friends. While there, I met with Peg and a couple of other women before heading to the Northwoods of Wisconsin. Arriving Friday morning, I rented a car and headed over to the rendezvous with Peg and the others.

I was a bit apprehensive, but as Peg met me at the door, her usual spirit of fun and kindness put me at ease. We sat down with the other women who were waiting in a comfortable room for us to join them. We talked a bit, and I told them about my friend and all the things I thought God had told me up to this time about the man that was in my future. Then we prayed.

What a prayer time it turned out to be. We waited on God, and he spoke again to me about my future and revealed, just as he had done when I was thirty-nine years old, that I was dealing with the untimeliness of a promised marriage.

> God was *still* foreshadowing a joyful love in my future and labeling the end result as, "best for last."

The main thing that touched me, that I remember still with fondness, was the word God gave through two of the women. He said he had "saved the best for last" for me. Seven years earlier, he had assured me that his timing for my life was different from the more common playbook. There was a man who was going to love me so much and was going to cling to me. And now, even though another half a decade-plus had passed, and I was now closer to fifty years old than to forty, God was *still* foreshadowing a joyful love in my future and labeling the end result as, "best for last."

As we walked toward the front door after our rich time together, Peg recalled to me her friends whose marriages had fallen apart in recent years. "Annie, hang on to these words God sent you today, that he has saved the best for last for you. He has more in store. Watch out for the temptation to chuck it all. Midlife crisis is a real thing."

I left feeling encouraged and knowing my anticipatory thoughts about my guy friend had been nothing but silly. I would stop entertaining vain ideas that God was up to any matchmaking. God had reinforced his promise to me once again that love was in my future and had added a beautiful frame. But God wasn't finished encouraging me on this weekend trip home.

Later that day, I checked in with friends at the locally infamous Fort Wilderness, a peaceful yet exciting Christian camp in northern Wisconsin, to attend a winter retreat for singles. At The Fort, having enough snow to cross country ski was virtually guaranteed. Other exciting wintery options included skating on a most romantic ice rink, built around three trees so skaters could do "double eights" around the trees, or risking one's life on a toboggan run that threw riders down the slope at what felt like twenty-five miles an hour, over bumps and through dips, to dump its screaming victims onto the camp's frozen lake.

More importantly, the retreat was organized by my good friend Teressa, and Teressa knew how to throw a good gathering, including finding an inspiring speaker.

This event was no exception. After we all found our way across the beautiful campus, snow-capped evergreens in all directions, we settled into a cozy meeting room for our first session. The speaker was a Wisconsin pastor named Darrell, one of many Christian leaders whose hearts were invested in the goings-on at The Fort. That evening, he was teaching about sharing our faith in Christ with others. But after Darrell took a short break and before he began part two, he threw out a sidebar pep talk that brought me back to the same message Peg had been sharing with me.

> Darrell: I'm looking out at you all and seeing that several of you might be between thirty-nine and fifty-nine years old. You're in middle of life, the time when a midlife crisis is a real possibility.

> Me: *I can't believe he is saying this.*

> Darrell: I encourage you in the halftime of your life— using a football analogy—to get into the locker room with Jesus so that you can finish the second half of your lives strong. There are characters in the Bible like Hezekiah, who did very well in the first half of his life but failed in the second. But then there's Manasseh, who didn't do well while he was young but repented, made a change, and followed God in the latter years of his life. The best thing is to have two good halves, but my point is that a good second half isn't guaranteed. A midlife crisis can throw it off. My hope for you, wherever you have been until now, is to make every effort to have a good second half in your life of faith! Don't let a midlife crisis pull you out of the game.

> Me: *Oh God, you are wonderful. Wow. I am amazed at what you are coordinating for me today.*

Darrell: I want to recommend a book that I found to be helpful. *Lost in the Middle—Midlife and the Grace of God* by Paul David Tripp. If you're struggling with lost dreams or feeling uncertain of your past or future, check it out. There you go! End of commercial.

I sat there pleasantly amazed. For the second time in a day, I was being warned that midlife crises are real but that I can spend this time praying to God for a strong second half. I did buy the book and read it. It was interesting to analyze midlife from the author's point of view.

> He was keeping the promise he made when I was seventeen years old that he would take the lead on helping me live a life of obedience.

But that weekend, putting it all together, it was becoming clear to me that (1) midlife crises happen to true and ardent followers of Jesus, some of whose faith does not survive; (2) I was personally not invincible from falling off the rails in such a crisis; (3) I had been tempted with an unrealistic vision for my future and had taken it into my heart to ponder; (4) sharing crazy thoughts with solid Christian friends is a good idea, and they can be amazingly grounding; (5) thanks to my friends' encouragement and arrangement, I had been in the locker room with Jesus today, during the halftime of my game, talking about my crisis of vision, and he was calling me to a good second half. He was even envisioning that the second half would be the best half; and (6) I should keep coming into the locker room with Jesus for the sake of following his game plan for my life and for the sake of what he would have me do for his kingdom in the remaining years of my life.

All of this filled me with gratitude and another round of amazement at the grace of God. He was keeping the promise he made when I was seventeen years old that he would take the lead on helping me live a life of obedience if I would just make a decision to do it. He was coming through!

Looking Back

It's precious to me that God met me where I was when I was tempted with a midlife crisis. He saw my situation and called me forward and away from the distractions. As I responded to his call to prayer, he gave me new promises for the future. He even labeled the long wait—by now you're seeing how loooong it was—for a spouse as saving the best for last. He made it into something especially good instead of something especially disappointing.

I think of Romans 8:28 and the strong conviction my father carried with regard to this verse: "God *causes* all things to work together for good to those who love God, to those who are called according to His purpose" (NASB1995, emphasis added). What a promise!

Twenty-Three

MAKING DREAMS INTO GOALS

Age forty-seven. It was a watershed year. The January experiences of 2008 with Peg, Dave, and the winter retreat were only the beginning of other things that followed in my life and helped me move closer to establishing a relationship with a solid man.

That year, I was twenty-four months into a volunteer leader position of a ministry at my large non-denominational church in Fulton, Maryland. I had been attending this church since 2005 when I moved to Maryland. Many singles had gone to the associate pastor, Mark, that led the church's small groups and asked him to resurrect the former, now defunct single adult ministry. I did the same, and he responded as he did to everyone, "I will gladly support any single adult who takes up leadership of the ministry. I'll mentor, guide, advocate. But I don't have the bandwidth to lead it myself."

For some reason, others had turned down the offer. For me, it was a natural fit, as I had helped lead single adult ministries at other churches, other ages. Also, I had established several programs from scratch in various jobs. It would be easy to recruit a team from a smart group of single friends that regularly met at my friend Kimberly's place.

And so, under Pastor Mark's mentorship, we shook off the dust from the church's single adult ministry and recharged it. Being ingenious and inventive, my team and I named it SAM for . . . wait for it . . . Single Adult Ministry. In SAM, we offered fun outings, teaching events, and retreats into the western forests of Maryland.

For one of our presentation nights, I invited an older single guy (I'll call him Bart) from the church to share a topic with the group. He accepted and shared on managing life as a single adult.

The man said a few things that I wasn't crazy to hear him share with those attending. His point of view harkened back to messages I'd heard as a young adult about the single Christian life. One of them was, "You don't need to go searching for a spouse. Don't use an online app or take up the effort. If God wants you married, he knows how to bring someone to your door."

Of course, the thought going through my mind was, "We don't apply this logic to other goals like finding a job; why apply it to a single adult wanting to find a spouse?"

He also described how he was able to serve better in a ministry at his church as a single adult than if he had been married. But I had been involved in all kinds of ministries enough to know that there are usually as many, if not more, married volunteers as there are single volunteers.

The message continued. "As a single, you need to develop close friendships with others to give you strong camaraderie in life. Find three or four people that you can rely on and who can rely on you. Cultivate those relationships."

This advice seemed to contradict his advice not to go looking for a spouse. If God should be responsible for bringing a spouse to your door, shouldn't he be responsible for bringing your friends to your door? Why would God give me the freedom to find and establish friendships to support my life but not the freedom to find and establish a relationship with someone that could be a lifelong supporter of my life—a spouse?

At best, the man's advice would make sense for someone who had followed Paul the apostle's steps for carefully and decidedly concluding they could manage and *wanted* to manage life as a single pilot. At worst, it was a regurgitation of the contentment message. After he was finished, I didn't want the group of younger singles to be left struggling with some of the same constrictions that I had once faced. So, I responded by sharing with the group, in the most endearing manner I could muster for the speaker's sake, that one of the three or four friendships they should feel free to establish to help them manage life could be a spouse.

Later, I analyzed the man's message with Pastor Mark. I shared that I didn't like what he had said to the group and why. As a background, Mark and I had something in common; we had both been involved with the same national, campus-based ministry in college, he about ten years before me on a different side of the country. In both locations and times, the ministry had the reputation of discouraging romantic relationships with anyone except the one that God was clearly calling you to marry. As a result, the group had earned the nickname "Never Daters."

But Mark had described to me earlier how he and friends on his campus had resisted the pressure to not date. They had seen dating as a healthy approach to getting to know others and to finding a lifelong love. Rather than expecting someone to suddenly fall in love with him for life or for God to deliver a spouse to his door, Mark trusted God to lead him through dating a woman to discern if they could develop a healthy and enjoyable lifelong relationship.

So, when I analyzed the speaker's message with Mark, he had many words of wisdom in response. And by the way, Mark was a pastor who knew the Bible extremely well. He was so joyful and jovial that someone could misinterpret his jokes for representing a shallow nature. This wasn't the case at all. He lived with both a strong dedication to God's Word and a wonderful love for life. He spoke honestly to me about the talk.

Mark: Annie, that guy is like other people I've seen. They get so involved with ministry that they make it the focus of their lives, as though the ministry is their spouse. So, you have to take everything he says with that perspective in mind.

Me: Do you agree with that lifestyle?

Mark: I think it's imbalanced. I agree with you that Christian singles should be perfectly free to date and to find a spouse. That's how I found mine! And I'll go further than that. I think that if marriage is an important goal to a person, they should feel free to make big decisions around that goal.

Me: Like what?

Mark: I knew a gal in college who was getting her PhD. This was back when fewer women went for PhDs than do today. She was smart; she knew she was smart, and she knew that in certain areas of the country, chances were low that she would find a man that could handle her having a PhD. So, she specifically moved to Washington, DC, where a higher percentage of men would have PhDs.

Annie: And?

Mark: And it worked! It's exactly what happened; she married a guy that also had a PhD. That was, what, thirty years ago? And last time I checked, they're still happily married.

Me: Funny how contrary that is in relation to the message of, "Don't do a thing; God will bring someone to your door." I mean, the gal you describe felt free to calculate in order to increase her chance of fulfilling her dream.

> She specifically moved to Washington, DC, where a higher percentage of men would have PhDs.

Mark: Yeah. Because she *was* free. God says all over his Word that he wants to support our dreams. And our plans. Nothing in God's Word indicates you can't treat your dream to find a spouse like a goal or a plan. Why should you be able to do that for everything else but not for this?

Me: Exactly! *Exactly.* Those were my thoughts listening to the speaker that night. That's the message that has seemed to hang over me since college—that marriage is something different, something I'm not free to pursue. My head sees my freedom, but my heart still feels this pull to an obscure thought that I am required to wait.

Mark: Tell you what, Annie. You live near DC. You are how old?

Me: Forty-seven.

Mark: And you live where the women outnumber the men by how many?

Me: I hear you. By a lot.

Mark: You want to get married, but you've never made it a solid goal. Just a dream?

Me: I suppose that's right.

Mark: Okay, well, there's nothing in God's Word that says you can't make a goal out of getting married. It doesn't mean you're cutting God out or doing something he's opposed to. It's his plan! So, think about this. Are there more guys available back in Wisconsin?

Me: I can think of several that are my age and single there, yes.

Mark: And here?

Me: Not so much.

Mark: So, what's to stop you from moving back to Wisconsin in pursuit of your goal to be married?

Me: Well, my life here is good. I have my sister, my friends, and I have SAM that I'm committed to.

Mark: Do your sister and friends want you to meet someone?

Me: (laughing) Yeah.

Mark: Would your friends move away from here if they found a spouse?

Me: Oh, sure.

Mark: Would they understand if *you* met someone and moved away, back to Wisconsin, for example?

Me: Yes.

Mark: Okay. Now, the last reason you gave was the single adult ministry.

Me: My good friend SAM.

Mark: Yeah, well, SAM is a not good friend if SAM holds you back from reaching your goal. (We both laughed.) Annie, seriously, don't do the very thing I was pointing out five minutes ago. Don't make ministry the focus of your life to the point of excluding your family goals. Jesus is the center of your life, the hub. And marriage and kids and ministry and work and exercise and everything else are spokes off the hub. If marriage is in your heart as a goal, and you are praying for help to find someone, then don't stay where there's nary a man your age to find.

> Don't make ministry the focus of your life to the point of excluding your family goals.

Me: But what about "Seek ye first the kingdom of God . . . and all these things shall be added unto you?" When it comes to ministry, that's the area where I especially know I am seeking first the kingdom of God. So that's the area where I am tempted to think, "Just wait for it to be added."

Mark: So, you don't believe in goals now? Haven't you pursued job goals and friendship goals and exercise goals without compromising Matthew 6:33?

Me: Yes, that's true. I've pursued the jobs and prayed to seal the deal if it's God's will.

Mark: And if I remember right, you moved across the country for a job. You came to DC *from* Wisconsin?

Me: Yep!

Mark: Look, all I'm saying is, please don't let something like SAM stop you from moving to a place where your goal can be better reached. There will always be somewhere for you to serve God no matter where you are. Don't be afraid to have marriage as a goal. Don't let the never-dater mentality and the contentment superstition cloud your thoughts anymore. Be free in Jesus. But give it a go. Think about the best steps you can take to find a husband. SAM isn't going to die without you.

Me: Where were you when I was twenty-one?

We both laughed but knew his message was important for singles of any age.

As we parted that day, I liked the idea of what Mark was saying and resolved to consider it.

"May he give you the desire of your heart and make all your plans succeed." (Psalm 20:4)

When renters in my house back in Wisconsin were moving to a new town, I decided to go there and work from my home for a bit while I changed from renting to a family to renting individual rooms to single gals. This way I could keep one bedroom for myself for whenever I came back to Wisconsin.

So, in June of 2008, I moved back to Wisconsin for a temporary transition but ended up staying. I felt so at home back in my lovely Colonial Revival home and was close to friends and family. Also, the firm I worked for had its headquarters in Milwaukee. But of course, there was also Mark's perspective weighing in on my decision. There were definitely more available men in Wisconsin, and I was ready to be more goal-oriented in establishing a relationship with a good man.

So, I stayed. And I'm so glad I did. Soon after, I learned that a long-time guy friend had bought a house in my Baraboo neighborhood just months before I came back to Wisconsin. This circumstance was going to change my life forever.

Looking Back

God used my conversation with Pastor Mark to bring me closer to my future husband. But the manifold work of 2008 was not yet finished. There was yet another tool—actually, a person—God would use to keep pulling me closer to the man!

Twenty-Four

THERAPIST SUCCESS

Age forty-seven. The title of the book caught my eye as I walked through the bright and lively conference exhibit space: *The Singlehood Phenomenon: 10 Brutally Honest Reasons People Aren't Getting Married.* In August of 2008, I was at a Healthy Marriage and Relationships Conference in San Francisco since I would soon be helping to evaluate such programs at work. The last thing I expected to find was a book addressing a core pain in my own heart. But God continued to bring along events and situations that were breaking down my barriers to marriage.

One of the authors of the book was Dr. Beverly Rodgers, and she sat there at the table. She and her husband, Tom, wrote the book together, based on their years of experience as Christian counselors and as owners of Rodgers Christian Counseling in Charlotte, North Carolina.

As I perused through Dr. Rodgers's book, I saw that each of the book's chapter titles was accompanied by a quote. For example, in chapter 7 titled "Reason #7: Wanting the Perfect Mate." The quote was, "I'm not a perfectionist; I'm just picky." I bought the book and chatted with Dr. Rodgers.

Me: It looks like you have a heart to help single people find a partner.

Dr. Rodgers: (warmly) That's right.

Me: And these ten reasons. Wow. I'm not sure what the reason is that I'm not married even though I want to be. I'd like to figure it out. (It was easy to be vulnerable with her, even though a stranger, because of the book that I now held tightly in my hand.)

Dr. Rodgers: It can be challenging to figure out. Even with a counselor, it can take a while.

Me: I saw a counselor in my thirties with the hope of getting help to figure out why I couldn't find a good guy. But she didn't want to help with my marriage and family goals. She said she wanted to help singles build a rich life as singles.

> Too many counselors don't support the idea of helping singles figure out what is blocking their desire to marry.

Dr. Rodgers: And what did you think about that? (I thought I saw a twinkle in her eye. She knew the answer.)

Me: I already had a rich life. But I was living it alone. Everyone tells me I'm wonderful, so I wonder why I can't find a guy. But the therapist's point of view reinforced an old message that I should be content alone.

Dr. Rodgers: It's an attitude I've seen in many of my colleagues and have tried to address. Too many counselors don't support the idea of helping singles figure out what is blocking their desire to marry. I ask them, "Isn't your marriage one of your best sources of satisfaction?" They always reply yes. So, I probe, "Why would you avoid providing professional help to someone who is trying to figure this out, who is trying to establish the same happiness that you have found?" This is what we are here for!

Now Doctor Rodgers had my attention. She got it! I said that I wished Wisconsin were closer to North Carolina because I could sure use her help.

Then she said six magical words. "Well, I can do phone counseling."

> To find love, you have to put all the risk involved onto your plate.

Long story short, I received counseling from Dr. Rodgers. Through a series of phone meetings and follow-up homework assignments, she was able to dissect in a handful of sessions what navel-gazing conversations with friends, over decades, could never uncover. As a therapist, she was an expert on relationships and identifying barriers to connecting with others. My sessions with her led to new habits that contributed to my husband and me dating and then marrying.

What was the barrier she helped uncover? It was an approach/avoidance conflict: I wanted to marry, but I also feared it. I feared that a marriage that started with love would result in rejection (probably came from some very early life experiences of feeling fully loved and then rejected). A relationship opportunity was a chance to love and be loved *and* a chance to be rejected.

Trying to establish a relationship (approach) stirred up fear of rejection, which led to subsequent behavior to eliminate (avoidance) the threat of rejection. To assuage the rejection fear, I could respond to a man's interest with too frequent of contact in an effort to assure myself that he was still interested and wasn't rejecting me. This frequent contact was panicky behavior that resulted from the conflict inside. I was unable to let a relationship take its course.

Well, everyone knows the word we use to describe such actions—desperate. How many potential relationships did I chase away because of my actions stemming from fear?

> It's funny to think of how we throw the word desperate around when we analyze others in relationships. "Oh, she was just too desperate." What I was experiencing was so much more complicated than desperation!

In one case, when a new beau and I were *both* contacting each other and getting together too frequently too soon, perhaps because we were both afraid of rejection, the whole thing fizzled out. We didn't have a chance to get to know each other's weaknesses slowly enough to accept them and assimilate them.

After the fall session I spent with Dr. Rodgers, I still felt the urge to call an interested man too often, but I refused to give in to that panicky feeling. I knew the pattern of chasing away a good guy had to stop. I learned to just let a relationship take its course. My approach was getting under control!

Also, I was less afraid of rejection because Dr. Rodgers had shared additional sage advice to calm the avoidance half of the equation. "To find love, you have to put all the risk involved onto your plate. You have to take the possibility of rejection, pain, regret, hurt, and a broken heart. You can't get to love without the risk of all these things."

I didn't like hearing her tell me this, but I understood her point. It helped me stop trying to avoid rejection but, rather, to expect it along the way to love. And it helped me be less afraid of hurting someone else too. This was some freeing stuff because a therapist was willing to help a person figure out her barriers to marriage instead of trying to direct her away from finding love.

My time with Dr. Rodgers rounded out a long string of situations in 2008 that had moved me away from a wrong response to my midlife crisis and toward responding to that time by moving confidently toward my goals for marriage and adopting relationship skills that would help me get there. What a year!

Looking Back

I can't say enough about how important it is for therapists to help their single clients freely address barriers to relationship success. We certainly accept the idea that people *in* relationships can get help from a counselor. Why can't people outside of a relationship also get help? If Christians who are married run into barriers because they don't have conflict resolution skills or relationship-building skills, why wouldn't Christians who are single experience the same barriers?

We all have blind spots. We're all vulnerable to pick up negative habits whether from families of origin, friends, or even from media. May God free up singles who want a relationship but can't seem to get there. May they consider the kind of professional help that Dr. Rodgers was able to give to me.

Twenty-Five

WHAT A NICE KID

Age twenty-eight. I met my future husband way, way before it would have been right to marry him—or even date him, for that matter. In my twenties, other friends and I joined in our church's big annual Christmas extravaganza that was replete with all the theatrics the directors could imagine (and the senior pastor would allow), including thirty choir members stuffed into a sixteen-foot-high "living Christmas tree."

It had at least one life-sized (seven-foot-tall) walk-through, pop-up storybook, and live camels walked down the aisles. There were twelve shows performed each year with a thousand people per show. They didn't go as far as to make us wear lit candles on our heads, but they might have considered it.

I had the privilege of putting a bike helmet under my belly and riding a donkey into the church dressed as Mary, the mother of Jesus. (On practice nights, another actor named Earl would grab the donkey's bridle and pull the donkey and me underneath the metal hangers in the hallway so that I had to dodge them and try to cajole him into stopping while I couldn't resist laughing! Fun times.)

> One night at practice, someone told me
> there was a new guy—just a kid.

In 1989, I signed up to be in the Christmas program as usual. One night at practice, someone told me there was a new guy— just a kid—who had been recruited to help manage the tech side of the program. The person described him as somebody who was super smart and creative and yet at the same time incredibly nice. This guy was amazed at the kid's irresistible trifecta of wonder! So, to strike up an acquaintance, one night while he was at the lighting control board in the church balcony, I called up to the young college student from below.

Me: Hey there! Are you Paul?

Paul: Yeah, hi!

Me: Hi Paul! Everybody keeps talking about how formidable you are, so I thought I'd come by and meet you.

Paul: Formidable?

Me: Smarter, nicer, and more creative than the rest of us!

Paul: Oh, well. I wouldn't go that far. What's your name?

Me: Annie Miller. I'm in the choir. Been in it for a few years now.

Paul: Cool.

We exchanged a few more pleasantries, and I walked away thinking, "What a nice kid." He was a teenager (nineteen), and I was a much older gal of twenty-eight. Paul and I went on to get to know each other a bit by talking from time to time. He was always up for a good laugh. I liked him a lot as a young, talented, funny, kind kid and continued to crush on guys closer to my age.

A year later, Paul was among the fifteen others and I who moved into the four apartments of the Gilman House. I got to know Paul a little bit better, but he was actually quite busy and away from the house a lot. I sincerely missed him because ... he was such a creative and funny and *nice* person.

Paul had a way of making people feel as though they had *no* faults. He wasn't one for expressing his irritations with people or circumstances. (He's still that way. At six foot three, he can cram his legs into the tight rows of a favorite historic theater or a plane row and never mumble a word about his discomfort. He says, "Why bother? What's it going to change?") When I or others in the house talked with him, his conversation was either telling us interesting things we didn't know, showing us how to make a beautiful object from Styrofoam, or splitting our sides with his wit.

He often cut me up with his imitations of Dana Carvey impersonations and made-up hilarity of supposed George H. W. Bush quotes from *Saturday Night Live*. Some of Paul's oft-repeated quotes were "Wouldn't be prudent—not gonna do it, not gonna do it" and "Thousand points of light." His favorite, and mine, was Carvey's idea of a Bush campaign trail assurance about knowing the ins and outs of the White House better than the other candidates that included such winners as, "I know the toilet in the Lincoln Bedroom will run all night unless you jiggle that handle!"*

Yes! Paul had it all memorized and could imitate Carvey impersonating Bush in the most hilarious fashion. Also, in the past, he and his brother Mark had made a few voiceover

---

* From *Saturday Night Live*. See transcript dated October 9, 1992, https://snltranscripts.jt.org/92/92cdebate.phtml/.

recordings of original Star Trek episodes that they showed us and had us all laughing. They turned galactic, life-threatening scenes into Captain Kirk descriptions of a broken pen or other mundane problems, all delivered with Shatner's intense emotional concern. One might say that these two were the class clowns of the Gilman House.

> Paul had a way of making people feel as though they had no faults.

As mentioned in chapter 10, the seventeen of us discovered over time that there were three sets of people in the house that had the same birthday. Paul and I were one of them! We were both born on March 18. He was born on my ninth birthday. I felt privileged to share a birthday with him. With our newfound birthday bond, he began to feel more like a little brother than just a friend.

The next year, I said good-bye to Gilman House. I still saw Paul at church events such as the Christmas program and even more through our church's young adult ministry.

One year, I tapped Paul to help me perform a song ditty I'd spontaneously written for a talent competition at a college and career retreat. It was a simple madrigal round that I knew Paul would know how to sing with me. And as expected, he caught on and improved it immediately. As I sang the main line, he added a repeating round in harmony. I even have a photo of us on "stage" performing the number, and that picture of us together from back then is so precious to me.

Eventually, Paul graduated from college and moved back to the Wisconsin Dells area where he'd grown up, but he would come back to Madison for a few months around Christmastime to lead the technical aspects (construction, sound, lighting) of the bigger and bigger Christmas productions. It was always fantastic to see him again and to have a laugh or two. Everyone felt this way about him. There was never a grumble!

Around 1994 (he was twenty-four and I thirty-three), I found him creating artwork with a scroll saw in the church foyer. I realized the craft was the answer to my desire to make a name sign for a program I managed. Eventually, the program grew into one that engaged dozens of college students and medical experts to go into schools across southern Wisconsin to talk with students about the benefits of and ways to delay sex. But it was in an infancy stage at this point, and I needed a lightweight sign that could be brought to events. As Paul scrolled through Styrofoam, creating beautiful shapes to later be painted and used in the Christmas program, I realized it would work for my needs.

Me: Paul! What you're doing? What kind of saw is that?

Paul: It's a scroll saw!

Me: That is so cool.

Paul: Yeah, it's amazing what I can do with this thing.

Me: Can you teach me how to use that to make a sign for a program I'm starting? We have our logo, and I want to make a five-foot sign of it to bring to events.

Paul: Oh, Annie, I can just do that for you. Bring me your logo. I'll blow it up and trace it onto some Styrofoam and make the sign.

This was *so* Paul-like.

It's important to know that the program name had two words. The first was in an italicized font and the second was in a roman (normal) font with block letters. Paul cut out both pieces, painted them black, added the orange underline that was also part of the logo, and mounted it all onto a big flat rectangle of more Styrofoam. I met him back at the church and was amazed at what he had done for me.

> Me: Paul, this is amazing! More than I could have hoped for.

> Paul: It was nothing. It was fun to use the scroll saw for this.

> Me: Paul, could you do one more thing for me? Could you just let me hear one more of your renditions of Dana Carvey?

> Paul: (in true Dana Carvey-esque George H. W. Bush fashion) Not gonna do it! Wouldn't be prudent!

In my scrapbooks, I have a picture of me holding the sign Paul made for me. Such a treasure.

From about 1993 to 1998, I'd occasionally run into Paul in Baraboo, which is close to the Wisconsin Dells. I didn't live there yet, but I had fallen in love with the quaint town and drove myself (and maybe a friend) there every month or so to hang out in a coffee shop and do some writing, window shop, or hike nearby. I knew Paul was renovating a home into a restaurant for someone (a slow process that took several years), and I'd stop by there to see if he was around to say hi. One time, it was our birthday, so I dragged him out to lunch with my friends and me.

It was always a pleasure to see Paul. He was such a nice kid.

Looking Back

I was twenty-eight years old when I first met Paul, who was a teenager at the time. Our age difference was a profound barrier between the idea of us dating. And it would remain for many years. At the start, we were Paul, nineteen and Annie, twenty-eight. Five years later: Paul, twenty-four, Annie, thirty-three—still a difficult match to imagine. In another ten years, we were Paul, thirty-four, and Annie forty-three. Getting more reasonable, but would a guy who was thirty-four *seek* a woman in her forties? He could still date someone twenty-eight!

When Paul and I did become closer friends, and my heart grew fond of him from a dreamer's point of view, I wondered if the age difference would be a perpetual barrier. Ah, but thanks be to God, it was destined to melt away with time, maturity, and friendship.

Until then, the age difference kept romantic thoughts about each other far from each of us. But there's a magical way of looking at our age difference at its beginning year. I think of my 1970 Christmas, the year I received the best Christmas gift ever. Besides the deep sense of joy that came to me that year, there was another gift for me under a Christmas tree miles and miles away. Up north in the Wisconsin Dells, in Wayne and Geraldine Wolter's living room, was nine-month-old baby boy Paul Wolter experiencing his very first Christmas.

If I know Paul, he was staring at the lights on the Christmas tree, taking it all in, and birthing in his heart the beginning of a magical approach to decorating with lights that would be matched only by other masters of the art. My husband has a way with lights! He's a premier decorator with anything. But he is magical with lighting.

> If I know Paul, he was staring at the lights on the Christmas tree, taking it all in.

As his parents gave thanks for their new son Paul and his twin brother, Peter, maybe they wondered about their futures and all that the boys would become. But I'll bet one thing— they never imagined that Paul's wife was living on the South

Side of the city of Chicago, already nine years old! Nor did my parents ever imagine that in the one year they couldn't give the gifts they desired to share with their children, God had given another family a baby, a *bonus* twin baby, who would grow into the man who would one day love their daughter Ann. (And one day, this baby named Paul would give their daughter a new version of the Battling Tops game she gave away that year!)

Twenty-Six

WHAT A NICE MAN

Ages thirty-nine to forty-six. Paul and I were destined to become closer friends, but it was going to take a while. In 2000, I had been working at the State of Wisconsin for a year and had saved up enough money to make a small down payment on a low-priced house. Trips to Baraboo had grown to feel shorter and shorter over time, and I came to feel a sense of peace and excitement about my goal to buy a house and move there.

As I began to look for my first home, I asked various guy friends who lived in the area to check out houses with me to help me assess them from a man's point of view (carpentry, electricity, structure, the things of which guys often like to collect and share data).

One day, I was going to look at a house on East Street in Baraboo that, according to photos and info I'd seen on the internet, finally seemed like the historical home I was looking for. I had looked at other homes my realtor had suggested or I had selected, even though I had misgivings, partly because they were the only houses on the market in my cost range. But this house had the Colonial Revival features of the 1940s—a lovely fireplace mantel, archway between the living and dining rooms, a built-in China cabinet, and most importantly, a big front porch with ample room for the porch swing I'd already purchased. In fact, there was already a porch swing on it with room for a second.

As described earlier, I asked Paul to look at the house with me. I hadn't seen him for a few years, but he lived in the area, and I knew he had been growing in carpentry and home remodeling skills for a long time. He'd likely have a thing or two to say about the house that would help me decide whether or not to buy it. And if he didn't, I'd at least enjoy spending time with him because he was still smart and funny and so sweet. He was such a nice kid.

But Paul the nice kid did not show up that day. In his place was another Paul.

This one was filled out, no longer so thin that he'd disappear if he turned sideways. He was manly and handsome. He'd never been that to me before. As I stood with him talking about the house, I couldn't help but say to myself: "Wow! Paul Wolter has turned into a MAN!"

Knowing me, I probably said it aloud to him. I definitely told other people.

> As I stood with him talking about the house, I couldn't help but say to myself: "Wow! Paul Wolter has turned into a MAN!"

I still couldn't imagine him being interested in me romantically, and I wasn't interested in him that way either. He was thirty years old, and I was thirty-nine. To me, he was still a first-stage adult, and I had considered myself to be middle-aged for a while.

Instead, Paul was a friend with a lot of knowledge and kindness who promised if I bought the house, he would restore the Palladian arch on the front porch, which had been covered up with siding. And that's what happened. Just as Paul had been there to help me by making a cool, portable sign for a program I was starting, now he was here when I started home-ownership, doing free work on my front porch to restore a beautiful architectural element.

One of my favorite memories, because it so embodies who Paul is, was a day when we were out on the porch while he tore down the siding that covered the arch and made me a new keystone to restore the right effect of the original design. I pointed out that the previous owners had installed a three-person porch swing that faced the front sidewalk. But I had a two-person porch swing I wanted to install.

What did he think of my taking the three-seater down and moving it so that the two porch swings faced each other, creating a place for conversation? I can still see his reaction. Before I could get the sentences out of my mouth, Paul was dragging his ladder over to where the longer swing was attached to the cedar-lined ceiling to take it down. He put the swings up where I wanted them.

Throughout the years I owned the house, he continued to be there for me, teaching me his unique approach to rag painting, taking down window treatments I couldn't reach, fixing my insulation problem in the west attic space, and many other helps.

One day, I decided to ask if he could figure out and fix why I couldn't get heat to the upstairs north bedroom (two heating professionals hadn't been able to figure it out).

Me: Paul, while we're upstairs looking at the attic, can you look at the walls around this room, the ones that have heating ducts running through to the north bedroom? Another friend suggested that the vent to this room breaks off from the vent to the downstairs bathroom, and that's why I can't get heat up here.

Paul: Wait a minute. Look at where we are and think about where the bathroom door starts downstairs and where that vent is. Annie, the vent downstairs is seven feet away from the north wall, and the vent to that bedroom is nine feet from the north wall. There's no way that the upstairs bedroom vent is branching off the downstairs bathroom.

Me: Oh, duh!

We went down to the basement to see if we could find the duct to this room. I had what some call an "octopus furnace," one that had almost a dozen ducts coming off it with a direct line to every room. My first year in the house, my brothers marked every duct coming off the octopus. There was no duct found that went to the north upstairs bedroom!

We assumed the vent in that room came off another duct. So when Paul and I went into the basement, he looked at the labels (and signatures) that my brothers had written. He followed each duct until it disappeared into the ceiling to assess if it was generally headed toward the room for which it was marked. Paul found them to all be labeled correctly. Our conversation continued.

Paul: Now let's make sure each one is truly opened. Wait! Why are the valve handles sideways? The heat is on, your house is warm, but the valves all look closed!

Me: That's their open position.

Paul: Remember that day we realized your cold air return and heating ducts were set up opposite to the status quo?

Me: Yes! And the valves are set wrong too.

Paul: The valves are wrong too. What a mess!

Me: Well, I showed you in the bathroom how someone installed the tub caulking.

Paul: Yeah, what was that again?

Me: It's a line of craters. The caulking forms little cups that hold the water.

Paul: Someone must have told someone to install it with their fingertip, but they misunderstood and instead of sliding their finger along to smooth it out, they poked it in with their fingertips.

Me: It's gross. Another thing that needs fixing. My house is always in need of a man's touch!

Paul: Well, back to the problem at hand. I might be looking at your problem.

Me: What? What?!

Paul: All the ducts are marked except for that one.

Me: Yeah, but that one doesn't have a valve. And it disappears into the center of the octopus, out of reach.

Paul: So true, *mon petite toute l'avec.* But look how it leads up into your ceiling toward the cold north bedroom!

Me: So . . .

Paul: So, climb up this step ladder and follow the duct into the furnace.

Me: (after doing as told) Oh my gosh! I see a valve hidden by the other ducts coming out of the furnace! There it is!

I opened the valve, and we ran up to the north bedroom. The heat was pouring out of the vent. After five years of not

Since the first year I knew him, Paul has called me, *mon* (masculine) *petite* (feminine) *toute* (feminine) *l'avec* (nonsense), which started because he knew I spoke French. What does it mean? Well, nothing. And, everything. It literally translates "my little all the with," but it could be translated, "my little darling with it all." Paul has never been able to determine where the phrase came from. My guess is it was from the cartoon character Pepé Le Pew, a skunk who was always saying mixed-up lovey-dovey French phrases. But it's adorable that Paul has had a pet name for me from the start in *la plus belle langue du monde*.

working, after two professional heating and cooling professionals had examined the problem, and after three different types of room heaters had been purchased and used, heat was freely coming into the room. Wow! Once again, I had a story to tell about how my friend Paul Wolter had helped me out when no one else could.

From 2005 to 2008, when I lived in Maryland and rented out my Baraboo house, even then, Paul was looking out for me. The wooden pillars on my porch were deteriorating, and he'd seen fiberglass versions for sale. He called and asked if I could afford them. If so, he'd grab them, and I could pay him later. He stored them in his brother's garage until the time was right to replace the old ones.

And so, from 2000 to 2008, whether I was living in Wisconsin or in Maryland, Paul remained a good friend. Not an intimate friend. Not a close friend. But a good friend. We did social things together, but rarely. I'd call him to do lunch on our birthday. But otherwise, I just didn't see him very often. But my friends did hear about how wonderful my friend Paul was. I even told them my funny story of how my kid friend had suddenly turned into a man friend. But even that was all platonic talk. I didn't analyze Paul to figure out if we were compatible. I didn't think about him or wish I could date him. But those days were coming.

Looking Back

It's fun to have photos of Paul and me in my first house from the day we walked around looking at the various rooms, the first day he looked like a man instead of a kid in my eyes. The day Paul helped me resolve my duct issue was classic Paul. He had and still has a knack for seeing what other people can't see. I have seen him gently and humbly correct several people in their own field of study.

A perfect example is the time a nurse was reading a post-op brochure to him, but she read it wrong. He had to clarify whether she was wrong or the brochure was wrong. When people ask Paul how he knows how to do so many things, he retorts with a laugh, "I can read. I read the instructions!" But he also just *sees* what others don't, as when he *saw* the unmarked duct disappearing into the middle of my octopus.

It was during days like the one when Paul fixed my duct problem that I would say, "My house needs a man's touch!" Eventually, I wrote the following song to express the hope of single women for a man's touch to fix their homes and to hold them in their arms.

Man's Touch

Unpainted porch and a clogged up drain
Rusty tin roof leaking in the rain
Fixing all alone ain't my kind of fun
My house needs a helping man to get things done

I need a man's touch
To push away the lonely
Move along the story of life
I need a man's touch
Talking 'bout forever
No more Mr. Ever Be Gone
I need a man's touch

Heading by myself to an empty bed
Hugs and kisses running through my head
Sleeping all alone in the deep blue night
My body needs a loving man to make things right

Strolling at a party underneath the moon
Couple after couple swinging to the tunes
Dancing all alone like a little girl
My step needs a leading man to give me a twirl

I need a man's touch
To push away the lonely
Move along the story of life
I need a man's touch
Talking 'bout forever
No more Mr. Ever Be Gone
I need a man's touch

I need a man's touch
I need a man's touch
I need a man's touch

Twenty-Seven

From a Dreamer's Point of View

Age forty-seven. Can you remember individual days, even the exact date that changed your life—your whole life—forever? As I mentioned in chapter 23, in 2008, I took a new work arrangement as a contractor for an associate back in Wisconsin and provided evaluation services from home.

That was the summer I moved back to Baraboo for what I thought would be a temporary stay. Renters had moved out, and I was going to re-establish myself in the house and rent out individual rooms to single gals. I had the plan to keep a room for myself so I could stay in the house whenever I came back to Wisconsin. But instead, I never went back to Maryland. Life just seemed better in Wisconsin.

Soon after I returned home, I discovered that Paul had recently purchased a house nearby. That wonder of wonders of a man, Paul Wolter, was living two blocks from me?! How cool!

Within a year, I was seeing him more often than I ever had when I began to help him with grant writing for the nonprofit he led. Paul was so kind to me—even-keeled, still as funny as ever. I continued to volunteer in other ways, in addition to helping him with grant writing. I'd help him do errands and even decorate the historical society's mansion. He was becoming a close friend.

On my daily bike rides, I'd peddle down the alley next to his home early in the morning, singing out his name—"Paul Woooolter!"—hoping it lofted up to his room as he was getting ready for the day and made him smile.

> As I compared Paul with other guys I knew, I began to wish we could date.

As I compared Paul with other guys I knew, I began to wish we could date. Yet, I didn't take my interest in him seriously because one thing remained: I was still and would always be nine years older than Paul. As I turned forty-eight, he was still living in the previous decade at age thirty-nine. He could legitimately date someone who was thirty-two years old. Why would he want to date someone who was forty-seven?

Paul and I began to make dinner together occasionally. I continued to dream of dating him but with no real expectation that it could ever happen. But he was a good model of the qualities I needed to find.

In the fall of 2010, I met a couple of guys—one was from Madison and the other from Milwaukee—whom I found attractive. Likewise, each was interested in me. They were both sweet and funny in completely different ways. And they each took their time communicating, usually going a couple of weeks in between phone calls to me. In my pre-Doctor-Rodgers years, I would have chased both of them away in the first month with phone calls to reconnect after a few panicky days passed without talking. But I was so over that habit. And truthfully, I wasn't interested enough in either of them because my interest in Paul was getting stronger. I wondered if God was knitting our hearts together. Could he be?

Since women often find entertainment in the love lives of their friends, other gals frequently asked for updates on mine. I shared my torn story about the two guys, and every friend would eventually ask, "Which one are you going to choose?"

I would always respond by telling them that I wanted to date my friend Paul!

However, I couldn't see myself saying anything about this to Paul. I was pretty sure things would become awkward if I did.

A good friend from work, Sara, was especially helpful as I dated the two guys.

Me: Sara, do you think it's wrong for me to date two guys at once?

Sara: Ann, not at all wrong. You don't know either of them very well, right?

Me: Right. But how long do you think this is appropriate? Honestly, I've never been in this situation before.

Sara: I'd say when either of them asks you to be exclusive, that's when you have to choose, Ann. Which one do you think you'd want to date?

Me: Paul!

Sara: Is that the Milwaukee one or the Madison guy?

Me: Neither. It's my friend Paul that I've known since 1989.

Sara: Well, have you told him you're interested in him?

Me: I can't. He's nine years younger than me. I don't want to lose the friendship by freaking him out.

Sara would laugh, and then we'd repeat the conversation again the next month. The guys would call me every couple of weeks, and this increasingly led to getting together. I continued to be interested in both but mostly wished I could date Paul, doubting that I ever would. Paul and I spent December working on decorations in the local historical society's mansion, where Paul ruled over a big Christmas shindig every year.

Paul was so exciting and had so much going on. After Christmas, we shopped for post-holiday deals, and I even helped him deliver a big gingerbread house he and a team had made as a replica of a real local historical home. Man, this guy reeked of talent.

On New Year's Eve, the Madison guy came with me to a swanky party in downtown Madison. Oh boy, he had broken the "meeting friends" barrier. People liked him, and it tipped the scale a little bit in his favor. Could I date him long-term?

Then I thought about the Bible verse God had given me a long time ago about the biblical character Jacob. He'd indicated that the guy I married would be like Jacob. I can best describe "Jacob" characteristics by comparing him to his twin Esau. Esau was a hunter; Jacob liked to cook. I wondered, does Madison man like to cook?

In 2011, January came along, acting like it was just another January. But it was actually a month that would change my life forever.

One day, in particular, shook things up.

Just before I went to Saint Louis, Missouri, to deliver a weeklong training for a company client, I received an email from Madison man that included the question, "Hey, you're not dating anyone else, right?"

Thank God that we didn't communicate too regularly because I needed space to respond to this. The time was upon me, the situation that Sara had predicted, when I had to choose between Milwaukee guy and Madison man. Fortunately, I could take a little bit of time while in St. Louis to think it through.

On Monday, I flew off to Missouri to begin training the next day. In the evening, I called Sara and shared that her foretold moment was upon me.

Sara: What are you going to do, Ann? Who's it gonna be?

Me: Well, I still have the same old problem. I don't have any strong desire to see Madison man exclusively. Maybe I have to stop seeing him and keep seeing Milwaukee man and hope a stronger attraction kicks in. His values are more in line with mine anyhow.

Sara: What about Paul, Ann?

Me: Yeah. I wish he were the one asking me to be exclusive. But ha! Since we're not at all dating, that's not a possibility.

Sara: I think you should tell him you like him, Ann.

Me: I can't!

It's important to point out that during all these months, I was continually praying about my friendship with Paul and desire to date him. And I was praying for wisdom with the other two guys. As I talked with Sara that Monday evening, I didn't know that on Thursday, something would happen that would shake everything up! It would also put everything in order.

January 27, Thursday evening, I came back to my hotel room after a day of training and called in to my personal voicemail.

Beeeeeep.

"Annie! This is Paul! Where are you?! Baraboo isn't the same without you!"

First, isn't it funny that we saw each other rarely enough that he didn't even know I was in Saint Louis? Second, wow! My heart thrilled to hear him say this. He'd never said anything like that to me. Perhaps Paul was getting attached to spending time with me!

> "Annie! This is Paul! Where are you?! Baraboo isn't the same without you!"

The next day, I traveled back to Baraboo. On the outside, my life looked the same, but inside, my heart was all stirred up! Madison man was asking to date me exclusively, and I couldn't see myself saying yes to him. Paul had missed me when I was gone, and this was driving me crazy. Would he be willing to date me? Why didn't he just ask me out?

I told Sara of this new development, and I'm sure you know what she said.

Sara: Ann, it's time to tell Paul! What have you got to lose?

Me: Sara, honestly, what I have to lose is my heart and . . . Paul's friendship. But . . . something about Milwaukee man and Madison man both being interested in me is giving me the courage to face the risk of rejection.

Sara: Yeah!

Me: I mean, maybe Paul won't want to date me, but hey, these two guys do. Dang! If he can say that to me, why can't he just ask me out?

Sara: Talk to him, Ann!

By Sunday, my mind was made up as I thought, *That's it! Enough with all this fear of saying something to Paul. Now that he left me that message, I'm going to take the risk. If I lose his friendship, I lose it. I can't keep this in any longer.* By Monday, I had crafted and sent the following email:

From: Ann Miller

To: Paul Wolter

Sent: Monday, January 31, 2011, 5:41 PM

Subject: A question

Paul, why do you think it is that you and I appreciate each other as much as we do but we don't ever date? I'm just curious.

I've got other guys asking me out (and I've gone and am going out with them!), but isn't it kind of weird that you and I get along well enough to feel that Baraboo is "different" when each other is gone? Or is that just how it works with good friends?

Paul, I can hear a squirrel scraping on the fireplace flue, and it is creeping me out! I bang on the wall, and still I hear a little scrape, scrape, scrape like it's trying to get in. Eek. I'm telling myself it is just working on its nest. :-)

Well, anyway, have a good evening! I need to make a priority list of all these house things. I want to get a new fireplace flue before tearing up the dining room. But we can do that insulation any time!

> Paul, why do you think it is that you and I appreciate each other as much as we do but we don't ever date? I'm just curious.

Now came the waiting game, and fortunately, I had learned to play it. I knew that what was *not* going to happen was me panicking and writing to him again. Instead, I sent a copy to Sara!

On Tuesday, I hoped to hear back from Paul but didn't. *Okay, maybe he hasn't even seen the email yet.*

On Wednesday, there was still no return message from Paul. I was a little bit hurt as I suspected that he didn't like the question and was feeling awkward. Hopefully, he'd find the words to say no gracefully, and we'd go through and get over an awkward stage but still be friends.

Thursday morning, there was no response, and I was sure I had lost him. I was truly sad but not sorry I had taken the chance. Dr. Rodgers had told me about the risks. She had said that on the path to love, I had to put on my plate the risk of rejection, pain, and loss. Well, here it was. I'd taken a chance and lost. It hurt. It might hurt more. But none of it was a reflection on my value. And besides, I was nine years older than Paul. How could I expect him to overcome a barrier like that?

In the afternoon, I opened my email and saw a return email from Paul, and my heart fluttered. I was glad he wrote back, but I took my time opening it. I was fearful of what I would find.

Finally, steeling myself for the likely pain, I clicked OPEN. And here's what I read:

From: Paul Wolter

To: Ann Miller

Sent: Thursday, February 3, 2011, 2:15 PM

Subject: Re: A question

Hi Ann! I got your question and have thought about it a bit.

In the past, I would have said our age difference was the reason. But hey, I'm pushing forty-one now! I don't think the age difference between us matters much at this point. Want to get together on Saturday and talk about it?

Paul

As you can imagine, to say I was pleased to read Paul's response would be an understatement. We had known each other for twenty-two years. I had been interested in him to some degree for at least a year, and now he wanted to get together and talk about dating.

> To say I was pleased to read Paul's response would be an understatement.

Something deep inside of me knew from that moment on, it was going to work out between us. But little did I know that God was going to give me a crazy "Godincidence" in the next week that would build that confidence even more. I was going to find out what the name of Jacob was all about in a most fantastical way on a most incredibly well-timed day! Meanwhile, I sent off a copy of his response to Sara so she could see that all her encouragements were paying off.

Looking Back

I would have never pinned myself as one that would write the email to Paul that I did. My desire was for a man to do all the pursuing, but for me, some of that was based in insecurity. I didn't want to take a chance at being rejected. If the two men had not been casually contacting me, I might not have had the confidence—albeit shaky confidence—to reach out to Paul. I see God's hand in the timing of it all!

Twenty-Eight

JACOB KISSED RACHEL

Age forty-nine. On Saturday, February 5, 2011, six weeks before I turned fifty, Paul and I got together for dinner to talk about dating. Both of us were a bit more animated than usual as we chatted over dinner. Afterward, we retired to my big brown, L-shaped leather couch, each of us sitting on an opposite end. We got off to a good start of awkwardly avoiding the topic we were there to discuss. But after a while, before more time could make it too difficult to get to the subject at hand, I threw out a hook, a very simple hook, that Paul took up and ran with.

I simply said, "So . . ."

Paul immediately assumed the lead, and through a short discussion, we decided there weren't any barriers to stop us from dating. Our ages, to us, were definitely a barrier in the past but no longer. And we decided that Tuesday the eighth would be a wonderful day for a first date! We would see a movie.

And that was that.

I made the necessary calls to the two guys I'd been seeing and let them know I was now dating an old friend of mine. They each took it in stride. No one accused me of deception or cheating or had a fit. Another indication that perhaps none of us were falling in love.

On Tuesday, February 8, 2011, Paul came over for dinner, and then we headed for the movie theater. We got to the parking lot, and since it was cold, Paul grabbed my hand so we could run together to the door of the theater. It felt strange to hold his hand after twenty-three years of friendship, most of which time I saw him as a younger brother. It was wild that my dream romance for the last year was happening after every other long-term crush over the years had turned out to be just that—crushed. But this was the real deal, and I was very happy to adjust to holding Paul's hand.

> We decided there weren't any barriers to stop us from dating.

But there was something more significant than holding hands that happened that evening that rocked my world. Years earlier (as I've shared), I asked God for a biblical picture of the man I would marry someday. His response was to read Genesis 29:11 that said, "Jacob kissed Rachel and began to weep aloud." I considered how Jacob had a twin brother and how the two of them were as different as blue cotton candy and a chocolate brownie. Esau was a hairy hunter especially loved by his father. Jacob was a smooth-skinned chef, especially loved by his mother.

Remember how I read this passage and surmised that God was saying I'd marry a man with inside skills more than outside skills? Maybe not a hunter, but a man who could cook up a good batch of chili?

But it turned out, these weren't the reasons that Jacob was a picture of the man I would marry. It is true that Paul is not a hunter, and he can cook up a good batch of *anything*. But more relatedly than all this, Paul is a twin and as such had some things in common with Jacob. I'd known he was a twin since about the year I met him. But on February 8, 2011, our very first outing as a dating couple, Paul began waxing funny about himself and his twin, which ended in his making a statement that floored me because in my heart was solidly lodged the Genesis 29:11 Bible verse that God had given me so many years before.

Paul isn't even one to talk about himself very much. But on this day, he told me how his brother was born many minutes before he was and how the doctor had previously asserted to his mother that there was only one baby in her womb, even though she was convinced there were two. When the delivery room staff delivered Peter and shortly thereafter discovered Paul, positioned feet first in the womb, they went into action. As soon as he safely could do so, the doctor literally took hold of Paul's feet with a tool and pulled him out. Paul likes to say he was never born but was extracted.

So, on Paul's and my first date—and me with Jacob in my heart as a picture from God of the man I would marry—Paul summarized his birth by comparing it to a biblical character. "Yep, I'm just like Jacob. I was born a twin, and I was born second! I was born feet first, and I kicked my brother out of the womb!"

"Oh wow, that's funny," I replied.

While Paul was cracking himself up with his joke about booting his brother out of the womb, he was completely oblivious to what was happening over on my side of the truck. I was stuck on the phrase. "I'm just like Jacob."

Did he just say that? What?! My spirit and mind were spinning.

So many years earlier, I'd asked God for a picture from the Bible of the man I would marry. God had said Jacob was a picture of that man. And now, on my first date with Paul, he had declared, "I'm just like Jacob!" Paul had never made that comparison to me in the twenty-two years I'd known him, and I'd never heard another man compare himself to Jacob.

> "Did he just say that? What?!" My
> spirit and mind were spinning.

As I sat there and heard Paul declare this, I sensed that God was saying to me, "Relax. This is it! This is the guy you've been waiting for, the one I've been promising all these years, the picture of Jacob!"

And relax about where the relationship would go, I did.

Of course, I didn't say a word to Paul about this until after we were engaged. No pressure! But it was sure fun to tell him after we did make that engagement promise.

God is amazing. I had asked him years ago to see his glory on the way he brought my husband and me together. He delivered!

God not only foretold that the name Jacob was a picture of my husband, but there were other promises and desires fulfilled too. When I was twenty-five years old and talking to God about my loneliness one day, he led me to a passage of Scripture that made me wonder if I would marry someone younger than me.

Also, one day I thought God dropped in the thought that I would marry someone who was a virgin, like me, something I hadn't been expecting, considering my aging self and the likelihood my husband, too, was living through decades of life to get to me. But it turned out he was.

I hoped and prayed that my husband's folks would be alive when we met, but again, as I aged, I was challenged to believe that was likely to happen. But Paul's folks were alive and well when we met and married. Paul and I had memorable times with his mom and dad in Paul's family home on most Sunday nights, whether it was watching *Downton Abbey* or enjoying a delicious meal together.

I had also prayed that my husband would be from a Christian family. Not only did this happen, but Paul's mom and my mom had come to know the Lord at a similar time decades before and through similar means. And as mentioned, they each had a habit of singing a song about God's love to their kids when they quarreled too much. They both became leaders in their fellowship circles. Both of our fathers, too, were strong believers who loved to talk about the works of God and to encourage others in their faith. They prayed over their children and hoped for them to follow in the faith. And they also both had a pull toward cottage industry businesses that have been fun for Paul and me to compare.

To have known my husband for a long time as a friend before dating was also a prayer and desire of my heart. I wasn't quite asking for a twenty-two-year-long friendship to turn into an engagement, but that is what I got!

> To have known my husband for a long time as a friend before dating was also a prayer and desire of my heart.

Another way that God answered my prayer to see his glory in our relationship and the way we came together was a fun thing that happened very long ago. As I've mentioned, Paul was born on my ninth birthday. And of all my birthdays through the years, my ninth birthday is one I clearly remember. One of my older brothers, *Paul*, the one to whom I gave the beautiful red and gold book, was away at college and living in a German-speaking house. As such, he wrote a note to me in magic marker in both German (drafted in blue) and English (the translation in red). The note was apologizing for not being home for my ninth birthday, but he ended up coming home after all. And I was thrilled.

I kept the note and still have it today and have always treasured that memory of my ninth birthday. (Sometimes I say to my husband, Paul, "I remember the day you were born," as if I were with his mom in the hospital! But I was far away, living in the city of Chicago.)

Most importantly, Paul was and is a man who is solidly founded on God's Word to guide his life, and he truly loves the Lord with all of his heart. That was the most important answer to my prayers for a loving man.

Looking Back

I made the commitment to obey Jesus as my Lord in 1979, thirty-two years before February 2011. What if I had known that it would take thirty-two years to start dating the man I would marry or that I would never bear children? Maybe I could have just relaxed over the decades if I *knew that I knew* the year I would marry. I certainly could have managed the rejections along the way a bit better—or just ignored men altogether! But admittedly, it might have crushed my seventeen-year-old heart to know this.

In any case, what God reveals, he reveals, and what he hides, he hides. And as a result, I was privileged to walk with him in trust and patience (and definitely some impatience) over many years.

Twenty-Nine

IF YOU MUST KNOW

Ages forty-nine and fifty. Paul didn't immediately tell his family that we were dating. He wanted to give our relationship some time to grow and be tested before getting everyone emotionally invested. He would go weekly to his brother's home to watch *Survivor* and didn't invite me along, and I understood.

The cat was let out of the bag, however, about five weeks into our relationship. The family's March birthday party was coming up, and Paul wanted to bring me along. It would celebrate the twins' mid-March birthday as well as their older brother Mark's birthday in late February and their dad Wayne's birthday in late March. Paul decided to clear it with his mom about a week before the party.

Paul's mom had been waiting many years for her youngest son to get serious about finding a wife. But he didn't show any sign of being in a hurry. He really didn't date much before our relationship. So, when he broached the subject, it took his mom by surprise.

The following conversation between Paul and his mom and the subsequent conversation between his mom and his dad were described in detail to me later by all three parties. They are precious memories to us. In fact, Paul told me this story a few weeks later as evidence that his mom—and not his sister, as I had surmised—was the person who was happiest that he was dating me.

Paul: Mom, can I bring someone to the March birthday party?

Mom: What? Bring someone to the family birthday party?

Paul: Yeah, I'd like to bring a friend.

Mom: Well, I guess so. Who is it? (She thought it strange, as he'd never brought a friend before.)

Paul: If you must know, Mother, I'm seeing someone.

Mom: Oh! You are!? Do I know her? (She couldn't imagine who.)

Paul: Yeah, you've met her. It's Annie Miller.

Mom: Is that the one who came out for Christmas Eve a few years ago?

Paul: Yes, that's her.

Mom: Well, okay, then. Well, sure! That'll be fine. (She was excited but was using the best nonchalant tone she could muster.)

Paul: Okay, thanks mom. I'll talk to you later. (He hung up and thought, *Well, that's done.*)

Mom: Okay, Paul. Bye now. (She hung up and went to Dad's woodshop to tell him that Paul had a girlfriend.)

Mom: Wayne! Wayne!

Dad: What, Geraldine? What is it?! (He sensed alarm.)

Mom: Paul, Pau, Pau, Paul . . . (She couldn't continue; she was too verklempt.)

Dad: Yes?!

Mom: Paul . . . (Tears were welling up in her eyes.)

Dad: What? What?

Mom: He . . . he . . .

Dad: Spit it out, woman! What happened to Paul?

> Spit it out, woman! What happened to Paul?

Mom: He . . . he's *dating* someone!

Dad: Geraldine, you just about gave me a heart attack!

Mom: We've been praying for him to find someone for so long!

Dad: Well, who is she?

Mom: That friend of his, Annie Miller, who had Christmas Eve with us two years ago.

Dad: Okay, so when are we going to meet her again?

Mom: She's coming to the birthday party next week.

Dad: Well, that'll be great! Just great. But next time don't give me a heart attack!

When I joined the family's birthday party the next week, I was added to the roster of celebrated births, along with Dad, Mark, Paul, and Peter. Paul's brothers and their families were clearly happy that Paul had a girlfriend. His twin brother Peter had been married since his early twenties, and for a long time, he had been hoping for Paul to find the same happiness.

We talked on the phone with his sister Cindy who lived in Upstate New York. She and I recounted how we had met each other some twenty years earlier through a mutual friend. And now she was so happy for Paul. Mom's joy might have come first, but Cindy was right behind her. Cindy and Paul had a special connection, and she, as well as her kids, had also been praying for Paul for many years to find that special someone. Well, I'd say that his whole family had been praying for this!

Over many months, as Paul and I continued to get to know each other better, we enjoyed cooking together, especially trying new recipes. We both liked to watch period dramas on our favorite streaming services, and it was such a pleasure to have someone with whom to cuddle. Or we would go to the movie theater. Paul said he saw more movies at the cinema while dating me than he had seen in his whole life. Or we would spend time together on activities of the local historical society where Paul served as the volunteer board president.

The summer after we started dating, I brought Paul along to a Miller family reunion. It has been our custom since 2008 to have a reunion when one of us eight siblings turns sixty, and this year it was my brother George's bash. All eight of us and most of the kids and spouses were there. No pressure! Paul had actually met my oldest brother Tom, who lived in Alaska, earlier in the spring. Tom had come to the Midwest for an uncle's funeral and made a special trip to Baraboo to visit me. So, Paul at least had one familiar face to see at the reunion.

> Paul was waiting for me.
> Or at least his family was!

My sister Barb and I recruited Paul early on to use his art skills to do a drawing for the birthday boy that the rest of us all signed. Baptized by ink! Everyone liked Paul, of course! And like his family, they were happy to see me dating someone I truly believed in. They had met a couple of guys before, and at least for one guy, some of my family had tried to talk me out of my misgivings. Thank God they couldn't. Paul was waiting for me. Or at least his family was!

Actually, he would say they were waiting in an external way, but he always expected deep inside to meet and marry someone. And by the way, Paul had been aware of various women being interested in him. But it had always been a situation of the wrong person or the wrong time.

One of our favorite memories from our dating years was deciding to work out together, most days, at the Baraboo Park and Rec Department's low-cost fitness room. Located in our town's civic center and former high school building, we not only used the weight room but also shed pounds climbing up and down the stairs. Paul's dad had attended school here, and as we ran up and down the three flights of steps, we pictured him running past us, up to his neck in shenanigans.

It was during this period that Paul got a divorce from a gal named Debbie. He had often met up with her at Menards when he went in and out of the store several times a day as a designer and carpenter. She was usually waiting for him in the checkout lane. You might know her as "Little Debbie"? She was bad for his health and had caused him to put on weight over the years.

But as we worked out, and especially after we were engaged, Paul said goodbye to old habits and cut Little Debbie and all her Zebra Cakes® and Nutty Buddy Wafer Bars® out of his life. He also ran fast on the elliptical machine as though he were on his way to something he would have loved to see—the last day of the World's Fair of 1893.

He lost forty pounds! I only lost seven. What can I say? I didn't like the elliptical!

Looking Back

We went to many more family birthday parties at Paul's mom and dad's home, both while we dated and after we married. We had silly fun playing sardines with the nephews and nieces or watching movies or playing board games. And Mom put on a spread at every get-together that was on par with any Thanksgiving extravaganza. Dad had a fun way of interacting with his grandkids that was a wonder to behold. We also went there on Sunday evenings to watch PBS's *Masterpiece* with his mom and dad. Wayne always giggled whenever there was kissing. So cute!

This was such a soothing time to my soul. My own parents had both been dead for more than eighteen years by the time Paul and I began dating. It was good to be in a full-fledged family again! These times were even more precious than I knew because about five years after we married, Dad died, and soon after, Mom sold the house and the eighty acres and moved into an apartment. It was good to get a taste of Paul's family life before it changed to a new season.

Thirty

FOAM CORE AND CHRISTMAS LIGHTS

Age fifty. After we dated for nine months, Paul proposed to me on Thanksgiving Eve, 2011. We were decorating my house inside and out for Christmas (yes, we start before Thanksgiving!), and he told me he was working on a surprise display outside on the porch. I had to stay inside.

My niece Sara had spent the night for our annual gingerbread house decorating party and was getting ready to leave in a few minutes. While inside with her, I confided.

Me: I think Paul is about to propose!

Sara: What? Why do you think that?

Me: First of all, he asked me last night if you were spending the night again tonight.

Sara: Huh.

Me: Sara, he just doesn't ask things like that. He doesn't pay any attention to who's coming and going.

Sara: Aunt Annie, I'm not sure *that* means *that*.

Me: Ha ha! Well, he has something up his sleeve for tonight, or he would never ask that.

The conversation I had with Paul was in response to something he had told me, which was that if I ever wanted to analyze him to talk to his sister. The deepest thing he wanted to talk about was what was for dinner. I had been waiting for the right time and approach to share with him that it just wouldn't do in our marriage for us to not talk about our personalities and expectations. He understood. And while we do have talks about the inner workings of the heart as needed, there are *few* times they are initiated by Paul! Such is the way of a man and a woman, at least in our case.

Sara: Hmmm . . .

Me: Also, he tried to propose last month, but I told him I had to have a conversation with him about something first, which has taken place since then.

Sara: Well, you'll have to let me know!

We said our goodbyes, and I asked Paul if I could walk Sara to her car and not spoil his surprise. He agreed and let us onto the porch, then he grabbed me from behind and put his hands around my eyes like a set of horse blinders, mumbling about the surprise I wasn't supposed to see.

Sara went into the street and around to the driver's side of her car. I saw her looking up at the roof of my house with a perplexed and surprised look in her eye. Paul, with his hands covering my eyes by this point, made a gesture to her, which I didn't know about until later, to keep quiet about what she saw.

We said more goodbyes through the passenger window as Paul kept his hands on the sides of my head, and she pulled away. Paul blinded me again with his hands and walked me back into the house, promising a beautiful Christmas decoration surprise. I sat in the house, talking to God about my continuing suspicion that he was about to propose, and the long row God and I had hoed together on the way to this moment.

> I saw her looking up at the roof of my house with a perplexed and surprised look in her eye.

A short while later, Paul called me out to the sidewalk, all the way to the edge of the street. I was excited and nervous because I was so sure he was about to propose.

Paul loves to work with lighting in a myriad of ways, and one of them is to use control buttons and timers to turn lights on and off in a moment or at a prescribed time. So, from the street, he pushed some buttons on a control in his pocket to make Christmas bulbs light up around the porch frame. Beautiful! Then he did the same to light the tree. Impressive! But suddenly, he started talking about having gone to Menards for some of the Christmas décor he was showing me, and my anticipation deflated. He certainly wouldn't be talking about Menards if he were about to propose!

But then, he added, "I have one more decoration to show you," and my heart skipped a beat as I detected a tiny bit of nervousness in his voice. He reached into a different pocket and clicked a button. On the right side of the lawn, a lighted phrase suddenly appeared: "Ann, will you marry me?"

Paul had drilled holes into a black piece of foam core and had inserted an amber Christmas tree light into each hole to spell out the question in lights. He had originally tried to mount the foam core on the roof. I learned later that Sara's face was perplexed because she saw the words "will you" lit up in Christmas lights. But the foam core was hanging and twisting in the breeze as the lightweight foam refused to cooperate with Paul's intended roof display.

I read the words, incredulous at Paul's creativity and that he surprised me after all.

> But then, he added, "I have one more decoration to show you," and my heart skipped a beat.

He looked at me as I read the sign and prompted, "Well?"

But I asked, "Aren't you going to read the sign to me? To ask me?"

He laughed and read the sign to me, "Ann, will you marry me?" I could feel his heart beating fast as we hugged.

"Yes!"

We kissed and declared our love for each other while Paul dug my engagement ring out of his pocket. He explained the design right away—while the engagement ring was a single diamond, the wedding ring would add an aquamarine stone on each side of the diamond to represent our matching March birthday. Every time I see my ring, I am reminded of our shared birthday and his creativity!

We went back into my warm house for dinner. And eventually, one of us said, as was our habit, "Now you get on that couch cause we're gonna cuddle!"

We had a very thankful start to Thanksgiving Day with his family in the morning! None of them knew ahead of time that Paul planned to propose that day. It was a joy to share the news.

We decided to leave the marriage proposal on display to cheer people's hearts, but folks began to ask me if I was going to show my answer. So, with Paul's help, I drilled my response into another piece of foam core, adding serifs to the font and inserting red lights instead of amber to set off the response from the question. My answer was a simple "Yes!"

Looking Back

To this day, we sometimes tell people the story of our engagement, and they say, incredulously, "That was you two!? I remember driving past that proposal in lights. We loved seeing that."

Thirty-One

FROM A LOVER'S POINT OF VIEW

Age fifty-one. "Reader, I married him."* Eight months after our engagement, seventeen months after we began dating, and twenty-three years after we met, Paul and I married on July 20, 2012, at Living Hope Church in Baraboo.

Four nieces (Christina, Brykin, Aleah, and Victoria) served as our junior bridesmaids, two from Paul's family and two from mine. They were so lovely in their pretty green and black dresses! My brother Mike and our dear friend Deb did most of the singing. Paul's sister Cindy and husband, Eric, joined our pastor in marrying us. We still remember the advice to spiral *up* and not *down* in our relationship and to see troubling situations with the distance of time.

Paul's nieces Natalie and Meredith and my friend Gail served as our ceremony readers. His nephew Zach served as an usher. My brother Pat, who had been like a second father to me for much of my life and the only other lefty sibling in the family, walked me down the aisle. My dear friend Liz served in the role

---

* I hope some readers recognize this line from the greatest Victorian novel ever written!

of my mom by lighting the bride's candle at the very beginning of the ceremony. Our sweet friend Tricia blessed us abundantly by stepping up as our wedding coordinator.

And do you remember the 1960s folk band called Peter, Paul and Mary, singers of "If I Had a Hammer," "500 Miles," and "Where Have All the Flowers Gone?" (I promise, I'm going somewhere with this.) The moment I first learned, back in 1990, that Paul had a twin named Peter, I dreamed of getting him and his brother together with my sister Mary for a photo— Peter, Paul, and Mary! But obviously, there would never be an occasion when our two families would be together so I could affect such a fun photo.

But not only did that occasion come, it was at *our* wedding! Peter served as Paul's best man, and Mary served as my maid of honor. So, I finally got my photo. Got it just by taking pics of the wedding party. As my mother-in-law pointed out, with my name being Ann, I served as the word "and" as we lined up: Peter, Paul, Ann(d), Mary.

> We each took our taper and, lifting our legs high so that all could see, broke them over our knees.

We decided to make good in our ceremony on a joke we started the night before. During our wedding rehearsal, after we used our individual taper candles to light our unity candle, we pretended to crack the tapers in half over our knees to declare our single years *finally* ended. And then we decided, let's do it in the real ceremony! So, after we lit the unity candle together, we each took our taper and, lifting our legs high so that all could see, broke them over our knees. Enough with these lonely years!

Also in the ceremony, I sang to Paul the following song I had written over the previous month to capture all the stages of our friendship over all the years.

The World of You

Back in eighty-nine, you were an up-and-coming leader
You were smart and funny, and you couldn't be sweeter
I thought the world of you
From an acquaintance point of view

A year went passing by, and you became a housemate
Your Dana Carvey antics made me laugh
until my side ached
I thought the world of you
From a sister's point of view

Through the years, through the tears
You've been here all along
We didn't know that love would grow
And bring me into the world of you

In the new millennium, you proved that you were handy
Working on my house and suddenly eye candy
I thought the world of you
From a woman's point of view

Leap to 2010, when you were now a neighbor
We made bananas foster; your grilling was to savor
I thought the world of you
From a dreamer's point of view

Through the years; through the tears
You've been here all along
We didn't know that love would grow
And bring me into the world of you

Here we are today; you've become my one and only
We say hello to love; goodbye to feeling lonely
I think the world of you
From a lover's point of view

I think the world of you, Paul, from every point of view.

Our guests loved the song. When I got to the words "eye candy," as our dear friend Deb the pianist had taught me to do, I paused, turned slightly toward the audience, and eyed Paul up and down with a sharp side angle. People laughed and clapped so much I had to pause the whole song! What fun! Paul made it more special by hamming up his responses to the words. Paul's niece Natalie, who had been praying and hoping for so long for Paul to find a wife, said that she was so choked up on the words of the chorus that she was ugly crying in the aisle. God had had her uncle's heart in his sights all along.

The wedding finished, and as we walked to the back of the church, it was such a joy to see so many beloved friends and family all gathered to celebrate with us. We went back in to dismiss each row of people and then did a second set of photo shoots with family after doing our first set before the wedding (yes, we saw each other *beforehand*).

Later, after guests threw birdseed, we got into our car and headed to the Chula Vista Resort in the Wisconsin Dells for our reception. We arrived and, with our wedding party, processioned around the room to the other side as Paul's cousin Jake announced each person. We again looked out on the beautiful faces of our friends and family and also the gorgeous flower bouquets that had been professionally designed and set on each table by our friend Alan.

Jake, who had had all the guests whip their napkins around above their heads to the beat of the processional music, had given us quite an entrance. He continued throughout the night to do a fabulous job as master of ceremonies and disc jockey. Even my brother George, who had attended many a big-city wedding in Chicago, was impressed.

Paul surprised me again by reaching in his pocket and clicking a button to reveal the same "Ann, will you marry me?" sign with which he had proposed and my response, "Yes!" placed up in a window above the reception hall.

We slowly got ourselves over to the head table. Peter and Mary, as well as my dear college Chuck, gave beautiful toasts to us and to our marriage. My dear friend Dave Hutchens prayed over our meal. And while we ate, Jake invited tables to voluntarily stand and sing a love song to get us to smooch.

After the dinner, we took more photos outside, and then Paul and I finally got onto the dance floor at 9:30 p.m. and danced our first dance as husband and wife. Later, after such a long day and a week of getting ready for it, we headed to our room for a couple of nights' stay there at the Chula Vista before heading to California for our honeymoon.

And so ends the story of our wedding day and the celebration of the wonderful love that Paul and I found after years of living life single. Thank you for coming along for the ride!

> And so ends the story of our wedding day and the celebration of the wonderful love that Paul and I found after years of living life single.

Looking Back

As this book is published, it's been ten years that my husband and I have been married. Like every couple, we've had our ups and downs and our own joys and disappointments, but we truly do grow more in love with each other every year.

For those who want but have not found such a lifelong love, I hope our story brings encouragement. May it inspire belief, hope, dreams, prayers, and the art of swimming like a salmon. And I hope that God will send personal promises and come along side you as a coach, as he has done for me and for so many others.

I would be remiss not to encourage singles everywhere to meanwhile cultivate relationships and joy at every stage of life. It's a pattern worth living on a daily basis. If a single person waits for joy to come through marriage, and if a person attaches to another the expectation of being their sole source of joy, that could lead to disappointment and even be harmful to the relationship. And hey, who wants to be someone's savior? One pastor friend, Tom, says it this way: "It's better to bring joy into a marriage to give to the other person than to come into it expecting to get all of your joy from that person. It's too much pressure on the spouse." Amen to that!

But none of that means we shouldn't seek the special joy that comes from companionship. It's possible to do both, to develop both your current life and your future life to the fullest potential possible. A pattern of just waiting for love to come is in itself another kind of pain, a hurt of helplessness. God forbid we feel no liberty to seek the kind of love God himself designed.

Speaking of God's design for love, I can't stress enough my conviction that the most important thing in life is to know the love of Jesus in a personal way. He was the long-awaited and promised Messiah who cancelled the curse of sin in the world and knows each of us personally and deeply. Much of the emotional and spiritual closeness I want in my relationship with my husband is what God wants with you and me.

The verses below capture things Jesus said that I find especially touching. For anyone that is of low faith and happened upon this book and made it through all my stories of faith, I hope you take to heart his words. At any time, we can draw near to God—as a child, as a single adult, or as a married person. Whoever we are, God wants to draw closer to each of us.

Can you hear him?

"Come to me, all you who are weary and burdened, and I will give you rest. Take my yoke upon you and learn from me, for I am gentle and humble in heart, and you will find rest for your souls. For my yoke is easy and my burden is light." (Matthew 11:28–30)

"Here I am! I stand at the door and knock. If anyone hears my voice and opens the door, I will come in and eat with that person, and they with me." (Revelation 3:20)

Acknowledgments

Many thanks are due to Paula Blackford, Tony Gryboski, Heidi Massingill, Nita Radtke, Kimberly Bronte Rigler, Cindy Walker, and Kimiko Miyazaki for reviewing my draft manuscript and suggesting important content edits. Thanks to you, readers don't have to read my long exposition and detailed description of what it means to be a eunuch! Instead, they get more details about Paul's and my love story, the focus of this book. I so appreciate this and other input that came from the time you invested.

WordGirls members group, and its founder, Kathy Carlton Willis, made an impact on my writing and finishing this book. I appreciate the consultation with Kathy and the monthly webinars and interactions with other members. Thank you for all you do as our Word Mama, Kathy!

Self-publishing is an elephant to be eaten one bite at a time. Published author and consultant Michelle Rayburn of Mission and Media provided the guidance and steps needed. She delivered the "boutique experience and personal attention" she promised through her myriad of design and editing skills. I truly could not have done this project without her!

Many friends walked along my journey of life with me, and I share about several in this book. Liz was one that, as a mentor, changed my life in a very deep way. Liz, I'm forever grateful for your friendship!

Thank you to my husband—Paul Woooolter!—for your edits and other insights along this writing path but even more for loving me deeply. I never dreamed that the name Wolter, as I sang it out in that alley, would one day be my own. Thank you for agreeing to our personal story being made public and for your patience in all the time it took me away from "us" to write this book. Without you, there would be no story to tell. I love you so much, *mon grand tout l'avec*!

ABOUT THE AUTHOR

Author and speaker Annie Wolter is a fun-filled Christian who loves to share and write stories of God's faithfulness and what it means to walk with him through the highs and lows of life. Having married later than she expected, she enjoys sharing her journey and encouraging single adults to turn relationship dreams into goals. She also draws from her experiences as a leader and speaker to youth and single adults. *From Lonely to Loved* is her first book, but future titles are swimming in her head. Annie is a contributing author of the book *Snapshots of Hope and Heart*, a 12-week devotional. She also spends a fair amount of time writing grant proposals and evaluation plans for worthy causes. Annie lives with her husband in Baraboo, Wisconsin, along with their two cats, Catherine de Medici and Diane de Poitier.

Visit Annie's website at **www.anniewolter.com**, where you can find photos of her journey from lonely to loved.

Write to Annie at annie@anniewolter.com.

FROM
LONELY
Loved TO

July 20, 2012